Challenging Your Worldview

in Search of a

More Excellent Way

Vol. 1

Marcus L. Davis

Challenging Your Worldview in Search of a More Excellent Way Vol. 1
Copyright© 2021 by Marcus L. Davis.
All rights reserved.

Scripture quotations are from the ESV® Bible (The Holy Bible, English Standard Version®), copyright 2001 by Crossway, a publishing ministry of Good News Publishers. Used by permission. All rights reserved.

THE HOLY BIBLE, NEW INTERNATIONAL VERSION®, NIV® Copyright © 1973, 1978, 1984, 2011 by Biblica, Inc.™ Used by permission. All rights reserved worldwide.

In whole or in part, this publication may not reproduced, stored in a retrieval system or transmitted, in any form or by any means – electronic, photocopying, mechanical, recording, or otherwise – without express written authorization.

ISBN: 978-1-7378981-0-8 (paperback)

Visit Marcus1Media.com to find out more.

To Thelma (my mother), Bobby (my dad),
Frederick K. C. Price Sr.,
and Alexander Sarraga.
These are the people who taught me the
most about living, understanding,
and improving my worldview.

I would like to thank you for reading this book, a work written as a letter of love in the key of improvisational living, searching for a more excellent way.

A portion of the proceeds from this book will go to
Reflex Sympathetic Dystrophy / Complex Regional Pain Syndrome
survivors, research, and charities.

1thousandrocks to take down RSD campaign and support

Thank you!

Contents

Preface vii
Introduction. xiii

Chapter 1   Making It Happen—Career and Personal Goals. . . 1
Chapter 2   Inner and Outer Declarations 7
Chapter 3   Intentional Listening. 13
Chapter 4   Loving Hard. .19
Chapter 5   Language—The Potency. 25
Chapter 6   Leading with the Arrogance of Ignorance 33
Chapter 7   Is Now Like Then—Can I Count on You?. 41
Chapter 8   The People Around You 47
Chapter 9   Money's Purpose. 53
Chapter 10 Picture Yourself as Offended. 59
Chapter 11 Breathe—Don't You Dare Hold Your Breath 65
Chapter 12 Truth—Narrowing the Wide View 73

Topics in Future Volumes. 81
A Brief Word about the Author 83
Scripture References by Chapter. 85

Preface

Do you think most people set out to provide answers to life's tough questions? I never thought of myself in that regard. But, for whatever reason, people often seek me out for advice. They want a different perspective on why they are unsuccessful in their business or personal relationships. Giving personal advice turned into my providing a service for them. With time and repeat clients, a pattern emerged—and with them, a common refrain: "Is this all there is? Is there something more…something better?" The result was this book.

If you've found yourself asking that question, no doubt you believe there *is* something better in life than what you are experiencing. Perhaps time and again, you've looked for wisdom and can't nullify the questions you have, or you can't formulate the right questions to discuss issues with your family or business colleagues. For this, I propose the following question: What do you use to reconcile (or internally negotiate) an answer to any problem?

Ponder this question: "Do I have a consistent way to solve simple or complex issues that arise in my life?" And can your way of doing so bear being tested—meaning the way you see the large and small things that captivate your attention. Open up, and let's explore.

As I listened to friends, family members, and clients, I began to understand why many of us have certain difficulties: the worldview we have is askew, or, at least in its application, we too often fall short. To redirect our efforts, we must consider the basis of our worldview to provide a greater perspective.

Everybody seeks advice—sometimes from a professional, such as a counselor, life coach, or respected mentor. And life has many opportunities for advisers to offer wisdom. Using the advice, each person navigates their relationships or business issues based on how they view the person giving the counsel and the issue at hand. Anytime we receive a piece of wisdom, it is necessary to understand the ultimate goal of the advice.

To grow in that regard, there has to be a challenge to your connections with people and the world around you. Because of this, many of us spend time searching because we can't accept what is happening in our relationships.

Your approach to decision making regarding your basic life principles requires a constant review. That also includes where you look for advice. Life's big picture will relentlessly fall on the small picture and affect daily decisions. In other words, what happens to an individual is a result of what happens to a community. And, because of that, any cohesive idea that is for us all and considered a good idea should be subject to constant review. If not, why not? Reviewing a good idea exposes its greatness and authenticity to all parties concerned—especially when they affect the family, the community, and the world.

Can your view of the world be opened and refined to get the best for everyone? Challenging your worldview requires that you draw upon several areas—culture, family, community, and country—because they affect each one of us. The goal of this book is to help you gain a better understanding that connects us all regarding the same experience here on earth.

One such aspect for consideration is that our daily events and relationships are interconnected. We observe others and see a plan of action they should take, yet somehow *we* do not. Too often the action is random and lacks focus for an overarching outcome. Yes, all of us will miss the mark at some point. However, the basis of our moves serves us best when we include the big picture: we are all living interconnected lives.

— Preface —

Over the years, while listening to people, I realized that most of us have something in common. While relaxing—and especially right before you fall asleep, you become your most authentic self. That is when you feel comfortable, reveal your promises, and accept the evidence of the day. Who is the person who accepts this as relevant and true information? You do (although, for many, the worries of the day are magnified right before sleep). Other times, you wonder and may even worry, and sometimes worse things happen. The challenges of the next day cause a detour in dealing with today's events in the best way, even if we intend to give it our best. The challenge is to connect yesterday with today and tomorrow. We do so to promote our most authentic selves. How is that done? We must examine our worldview. For example, how you handle any intense event must be connected, in a healthy way, to any relaxed event in life's journey.

Sometimes you think you are going to change. And then something happens to today's decisions when tomorrow arrives. Other times you just let the days roll by never intentionally moving toward better days. You are not different because of your culture. Every culture, major and minor, throughout the world's history, does not look at the future the same, nor do they always consider their past to reflect their major values. It's necessary to have a basis for existence that allows everyone to pursue a future most coherent to what we, as people, have experienced thus far and desire moving forward.

Our reasoning has breakable barriers, and we need guardrails to keep us in line. No two people, given the same circumstances—whether of different backgrounds or similar cultures—arrive at the same understanding consistently. Yet there is no excuse for leaving a certain measurable reality. Everyone shares a commonality that we cannot ignore. As such, critical thinking is a necessity. If we are so confident of many things outside our grasp, we most definitely can arrive at things within our grasp. The content of this book engages those who want to anchor their thoughts for the best outcomes in more areas of their lives—and to fully rest. Receiving advice along with a proper vision of the world provides greater success.

Accepting that there is more for you is the proper perspective to go through life's journey with clarity and the richness of peace. No other person can do it for you. Only you can work through those measures, with the help of others. What we know from examining our community is that others also work toward a goal. When you ask yourself, "What are my most important goals?" often too much focus is on the follow-through, and while that is essential, you must have a basis for the ideas you desire to rectify.

Now is the time to challenge your vision and solidify how you will know when you see success in your home or place of work. In this book, you will be able to follow questions and examples to help guide you through your worldview. As you reflect upon these concepts, you will work toward peace.

If the basis of your philosophy is corrupt, it may determine whether you can rest at night. Moreover, it may determine if you allow your household to rest. Everyone's fundamental view toward others needs refinement. As we age, we should obtain wisdom. The main issue is when you do not seek additional understanding throughout your life's journey outside your immediate surroundings. An unchallenged worldview will result in less triumph.

Sometimes we need a push, a reimagining of what we believe to be in line with what we do. This book reads with the intent to do that very thing. It examines how you interact with your family and colleagues according to your worldview—and not just your worldview, but also your application of it. What if you realized that what you always thought was true was never going to work as you interact with others? Then it's acceptable to say you will want to discover a better way. That's what a lot of folks seek when they pay a consultant, seek a life coach, go for advice, or get counseling. It is not a place of shame.

Many sciences offer views that can provide clarity to a particular circumstance you or someone else is facing. However, there still needs

— Preface —

to be a backstory of conclusions that involves all people working toward a better way. In writing this book, I reviewed different approaches and worldviews to solving issues. My direct aim is to challenge you and also to allow you to reconsider your decisions as self-serving or serving everyone. Some of what is written in this book may be hard to accept. That is the point.

The important thing to remember, as we examine your worldview, is to ask questions about the *application of your worldview.* The common human experience happens whether we give credence to it or not.

Whatever your worldview—and many state there are several—it boils down to:

> *Are you in this life with me or are you against me, and is the basis for your claim one that I can rely upon?*

It's evident that you have a basis for your claim by your defense.

In this book, a worldview is determined by your understanding of inevitability, conclusions, and decisiveness as you embark on life's journey. My intent is to help you increase your confidence in what you believe thus far and open your understanding to refining it for the best outcomes. Our worldview is either informed, or it is not. It's a journey that promotes an ongoing investigation, collection of information, and use of know-how.

In short, an appropriate worldview is one that seeks and develops a more excellent way (1 Corinthians 12:31).

Introduction

Challenging Your Worldview drives a particular perspective: everyone seeks advice looking for the best answers to whatever life has for them. Yet the fundamental part of seeking advice is to reconcile the purpose of the advice in the first place. The original intent can get lost if you don't understand how we receive and act upon the advice. More than that, it's vital to understand the origin of that advice and how it impacts your overall life, not just the particular moment you are living through.

The chapters in this book are intended to examine your views, redirect them for consideration, and ultimately provide principles for better living. Further, the questions posed will allow you to express thoughts you desire to say to a loved one or coworker for a more productive life. We all face hurdles and subjects that must be tackled at home, in our relationships with people outside the home, and in the workplace. Just know there is always help.

To apply advice, questions about feelings are necessary, and that is why many advisers and counselors pose various questions. Those questions ultimately spur us to better solutions. Critical thinking is needed to work through any situation you may face, positive or negative. Questions provide perspective and food for thought for the adviser and the person seeking answers. The questions you'll find in this book are intended to challenge you in unexpected ways. For example, in chapter six I pose the question: What does leading a family astray mean? Most of us never consider whether we are unintentionally leading our families to hardship.

Another question, on the subject of offending others (chapter ten), asks you to think about "How can I be responsible?" Anyone can passively or proactively offend other people. How you live and what you do can offend colleagues or the people you love. Is it possible you are unwittingly an offensive person? Better yet, is it possible you can become less offensive so that you live a more peaceful life? You can't fix another person's perspective; however, your example goes a long way. Seeking wisdom in redirecting your worldview about offense is not an attempt to overcome their views. The chapter will help you consider how we are all connected and how our actions can work together for the good of everyone.

Now let's discuss what this book is *not* intended to do. Like any book, it will not replace the need for human interaction with someone who has a healthy worldview. To that claim, I say this: seeking advice means you believe there is a proper way to live that overrides every other perspective you currently have. Total submission to the principles is difficult if you've never heard of them or their explanations. This book is not a substitute for any other writings, but it will help you to explore. Holistically, the Bible is finished and should be read as a complete work. Yet the holy writings mandate that you interact with others and grow in wisdom. Challenging your worldview accentuates that need. Moreover, this book is not intended to drive science out of your worldview. Spiritual writing and science are companions (hint: the origin of the word *science* is actually one aspect of the spiritual).

The book of Proverbs explains which direction a person can take to flourish in life. It encourages the reader to consider a different way to go about life. This book offers questions about your worldview considering the science of applying principles from the different disciplines in advising others. Although you can get a lot from reading this book alone, I urge you to apply the ideas to receive a better understanding. The intention is for you to interact with others in the application and also in conversation. Interaction with others will increase the significance of what you read.

← Introduction →

One opportunity to interact is found in chapter seven. It discusses the reality of forgiveness. Many people have a hard time forgiving and still deal with remembering the incident. So they question the effectiveness of forgiving. Honestly, every one of us needs forgiveness, and this book seeks to help you release yourself or others from responsibility to the detriment of yourself. That is only part of seeking a more excellent way and is not the full picture of a complete worldview.

Challenging Your Worldview has three main objectives:

1. Question your personal and public values on different topics to see if they align with one another.
2. Redirect your hopes and goals to set them up with a worldview that goes along with what you say and do.
3. Arrest your current worldview long enough to think critically about the next chapters in your life. Those who are looking for a better way to understand personal and business relationships will find each chapter in this book to be a highlight of information relevant to now and the future they desire.

Chapter 1

Making It Happen—Career and Personal Goals

It's good to have a measure of success. Everyone wants to feel they accomplished something in life whether they work for a company, are self-employed, or serve as a homemaker. Too often our accomplishments render an internal fear or pride that shows up to others as anger. We do this when we expect others to buy into our accomplishments, and when they do not, we become angry. Also, our perspective of what is happening becomes a distraction that takes away from our achievements. One alternative idea is to understand that life is a journey full of goals, and we are to embrace them large and small.

Questions:

- What do you want your accomplishments to prove?
- Who do you need the most approval from when you accomplish something?
- Will you ever arrive at your goal and know exactly what it looks like?
- Do you need to arrive at your goal to be satisfied?

After all your training, whether it's brief and hands-on or several years at multiple institutions, the work you do can bring a great deal of satisfaction—and you are doing it well. The pay you receive is never enough, yet somehow you make do. You measure your work against others and say to yourself, "I'm okay…maybe I'll ask for a raise next year." What we all secretly hope is that our supervisor will see our work ethic and pay us what we deserve. Of course, for most people that never happens.

Does it matter? Our perspective may change when we consider this passage from Colossians 3:23 (ESV), "Whatever you do, work heartily, as for the Lord and not for men." To tell the truth, what we do is for us—yes, us, men and women alike. The household we must maintain is an important part of our pride schedule. I say schedule because accomplishments can be long-term or short-term, such as managing our diet or buying our best friend dinner while they struggle to build their business.

As you work heartily, never forget the basic advice for the industry where you work so hard to see your success. You, as a member of that industry, were drawn to it, possibly because of a relative, or perhaps it's where you spent much of your youth. Like many, time with your older siblings doing things such as cleaning up a construction yard after your dad's labor may make you want to own the construction business. That is until you realize you would rather paint the buildings or create a clean-up business for construction crews. What you find is that your perspective leans toward a place of belonging. The proper marketing strategy—that is to say, what you sold yourself—is a basic message of accomplishment that feels safe. The job is worthy of your work, time, and creativity. We can rest "Knowing that from the Lord you will receive the inheritance as your reward," as it says in Colossians 3:24 (ESV). "You are serving the Lord Christ" with your whole being, and that is no small task itself. Our accomplishments improve our way of living and suggest to our Savior that we understand.

If you do not see the success you desire, remember this advice from the apostle Paul: "Not that I am speaking of being in need, for I have learned in whatever situation I am to be content" (Psalm 4:11, ESV). That is not an excuse. It is simply a moment of reflection. The journey is worthy of respect and joy—many times even more so than the goal itself. To keep goals in perspective, ask yourself, "Do I want the goal or the journey?" Both have merit as you realize the journey is respected by many and the goal is simply the celebration of a journey well spent.

Any accomplishments have their place and limits. No one said you have to arrive tomorrow unless the ultimate goal has a specific expiration. Meeting deadlines for personal growth is a matter of choice, not the force of others. Too many succumb to listening to the goals of others to see how they measure up. Guess what? You will never measure up once you dig deeper into their motivations and outcomes. Comparing yourself to your child or your grandmother will get you off-track with your goals. A personal meeting with yourself and your main counsel sets your goals. No one can eradicate your movement when proper motivations are set in place.

For example, many people run a marathon to win. Others run in support of a cause. Yet another runs simply for their personal best. Still another runs the race to prove to themselves they can do something big. All these runners are on the same track with differing intended outcomes. Because of a healthy attitude, many of them support one another and do not get in the others' way. Notably, the other runners may be unaware of the competitor's intentions.

Okay, time now for a reality check. Who said a goal is something to relish? Is it the world or you that makes the decision? Certainly you and only you are the authority of your goals. No other *person* can offer a goal for you, but God can. He is the perfection we seek in the form of Jesus. Goals need to be in line with God's view of our world. Moreover, the view of God means we are in line with what plans land us squarely in His path. Writing to his spiritual son, Timothy, Paul says, "But godliness with contentment is great gain" (1 Timothy 6:6,

ESV). No matter where you are on the journey, adding insight to the heavenly Father's will brings peace to your life.

There is a secret sauce to "making it happen," and it's called "being and doing." It's a recipe to move wholeheartedly toward your goals and contentment—to be where you are supposed to be. That includes being there at the appointed times prepared to participate. If the coach tells you to show up ready to do several laps, you don't want to be the one who gets there with your running shoes still at home. Much worse, the instructions told you to stretch because the arrival of the coach means the running starts. Being where you are supposed to be means preparing to make it happen by getting to the point of doing.

The doing part of the recipe is where many get stuck. Because of a lack of respect for the smaller goals, many get overwhelmed. Take it the same way you eat an elephant or construct a dinosaur after discovering its bones—one section at a time. Smaller goals in the "doing" part of the recipe make us stronger and better-prepared goalkeepers. Do the smaller tasks over and over until you know you are ready to fulfill the next step. Set limits so that you move on, and do not do it in a vacuum. Proverbs 15:22 (ESV) teaches, "Without counsel plans fail, but with many advisers the plans succeed."

You will get there in your private and personal journeys. In perspective, both a goal and the journey are worthy of respect. Neither one is worthy to the detriment of your main goal. Ask yourself, "What is the main goal for my personal and business life?" If the answer doesn't resemble something that serves a particular purpose with or without your business intact or your personal life being sound, then you missed the reason for a sound plan to make it happen. The most definitive plan in business is making money and keeping the doors open for a specific purpose. In your personal life, the goal is a successful home life with family and friends and being healthy so you can enjoy them to the fullest.

Making It Happen—Career and Personal Goals

To what end is that fulfillment if anything takes a turn? That understanding is the journey we seek in being content and joyful about our goals. It is serving the purpose we are excited to join, and that is serving the greater good of all of us in our communities that make up the world.

Chapter 2

Inner and Outer Declarations

Each of us wears many masks to hide from our family, fellow believers, colleagues, and ourselves. The façade comes in the form of hoping for the best when we know nothing is truly being done. Observation tells you that no one is speaking, praying, or planning for a change. Such a realization is heartbreaking. If you are honest, you can acknowledge that no one is acting in any real sense by their declarations. The results are an unfulfilled future wanting the past to change because what we could declare today never took place.

Questions:

- Are you ready to tell others what you declare for yourself?
- How do you feel when you make a declaration?
- Are inner declarations important too?

Does your inner and outward declaration match? How often do you affirm to yourself, when alone, what you say to others? Many times these two forms of thinking are not working together. As a result, they are working against one another. For example, when your children see you, they should be excited and see you as a form of hope and security. Moreover, coworkers and friends should expect the same in your conversation and tone. As a parent, your language cannot suggest that you have to babysit your children. That mindset is often seen as a chore or burden. Taking care of your children is a privilege and honor. While doing so, you can form their declarations as they explore the world.

Since the beginning of recorded time, people have loved to deceive one another. The blame goes in many different directions. And personal blame should sit on the table with all the others that you argue are to blame. If you don't share in the blame, why are you not showing others how to maintain a blameless life in regards to outward and internal deceit? How you feel about it is of no importance. Your feelings will sway your alignment toward proper inward or outward declarations. What you say and act upon matters more than how you feel. The reason is because our feelings can change; however, once we speak to ourselves and others, it takes ahold of the person receiving the message.

To understand our outward affirmations, adjudications, reformations, propagations, and perpetuations we must consider the most personal basis of our inward declarations. What was capturing your imagination so much that you were bound from free-flowing thought? Are you unable to discover what is best for you and the family because you are not free? The choice to ignore this freedom of truth is ever-present. It hurts so many especially if their lifestyle demands deception. However, we can trust this passage: "Now the Lord is the Spirit, and where the Spirit of the Lord is, there is freedom" (2 Corinthians 3:17, ESV). Deceiving yourself is the first step to stifling growth. Are you able to tell others what you affirm to yourself?

← Inner and Outer Declarations →

Here is an easy exercise to do. Find someone on television or another video platform that you don't agree with in their assessment of a particular topic. Write down three main points they discuss. Contemplate those topics for a few days and then return to them and write supporting viewpoints. To add to that, write what you would affirm out loud to others concerning the three major points. When choosing this topic, make sure it's something you are willing to share. What you write about the topic in support is not relevant to share. It's an exercise in declaring to others what you would say to yourself. After doing so, listen to your spouse and coworkers with the same intent. Hear what they're saying as though you have to support it with your affirming language. The intent is to see if you can support their thought processes with outward declarations. Family and business relationships need cohesion to continue.

Declare out loud that you are going to be a person living in peace. Accept nothing less when it comes to being honest with yourself. Your affirmations about now and the future do not need judgment. They need a decision based on reliability. What you promote needs clarity about the truth.

Consider if your child comes to you and repeats something about a neighbor that you said a week ago. Now you know what you said is untrue. Your child, however, says they witnessed it. The claim is impossible without a miracle. What are you to do now? Do you draw a line in the sand and punish the child for apparent deception? You circulated the deception, and your child picked up on it and ran with it. Just then the doorbell rings. It's another neighbor with their child telling you the lie that went through your child into the ears of others and landed with the neighbor at your door. The neighbor wants your child punished before it gets to the neighbor about which the lie was told. What are you to do as the one whose mind is at fault because you let your rest be disturbed by perpetuating a mistruth? Do you now just restructure the deception to protect your household and personal embarrassment? Integrity is at play and perfect peace is now questionable. You are the parent of a liar. That can never be okay with you and the hopes you have for your family. A steady, faithful reputation is reliability in what we declare, not how we feel.

Outward declarations should match our deepest understanding. If we lie to ourselves, what do we give others? A mask of deception can hurt our existence if we continue to work toward inward deceptions. They eventually cause harm to others. Proverbs 18:21 (ESV) reminds us, "Death and life are in the power of the tongue, and those who love it will eat its fruits." Loving life means minding our deceitful actions. It is the way to reconcile a peaceful life. Matthew 12:37 (ESV) adds, "For by your words you will be justified, and by your words you will be condemned." Proper rest comes from a foundational belief that inside you learn and study the truth. The result is peace so that you do not promote unrest in the world by deception. The last chapter of this book explores more insight concerning truth and integrity.

For those who exclaim, "Well, that's fine, but how do I know what is real?" I challenge you to declare things that are helpful in every situation. I suggest, in a time with books and videos at your disposal, that you listen to people who don't agree with you. Also, listen to those who arrive at the same conclusion as you with a different worldview. In this continual study, you can find what affects everyone and also what the lasting results are. Do they affect everyone differently? A rocket scientist may say something different about gravity, for example, from a hang glider. They have opined a different perspective on gravity. They have not discovered it doesn't exist. All of us deal with the results. Therefore we must acknowledge it in every situation.

What we declare is not based on putting our feelings first. It is better if we put harmony at home and in the workplace first. That is not to excuse what we allow. It means using how we declare something to be a positive versus a negative. Any explicit announcement must contain three things: awareness, the future, and honesty. You need to be aware of all appropriate information about what you declare and what its implications are, then be able to rest fully as the truth always prevails.

← Inner and Outer Declarations →

The good news is that results are evolving for all of us. Anything you declare now may change as you have the opportunity to grow in understanding. "The beginning of wisdom is this: Get wisdom, and whatever you get, get insight" (Proverbs 4:7, ESV).

When would you say you are your most authentic self? Is it when you wake up before the worries of the day hit you? It could be when you are away from everyone and you find peace because no one can disturb you. Right before you fall asleep, you must feel secure to turn off the worries of the day. Our most authentic self is what we declare and disclose to ourselves when no one is able to listen. A peace that surpasses all understanding, as touted in Philippians 4:7, marks the mindset of a person who delivers fewer harmful declarations. They feel at peace.

Lying brings night terrors (not the only reason). And, no, I don't mean dreams. Do you want to sleep in the same house with people who daily lose respect for you because of your lies? Whether simple, big, small, or "understandable," lies are all inward declarations for disaster. First you think it and then you act it out. Consider if you want to sleep next to a spouse who never sets the coffeepot and checks the door after they are up late working. Yet they always tell you they did. After a couple of months, what are your thoughts about the coffee and the door? Do you reconcile that the door didn't need to be locked and that you can make your own coffee? Those things will likely become someone else's duty. However, you now need to contend with the deception of the person with which you share a home. The same goes for you if your inner thoughts practice outward deceptions.

Isaiah 26:3 teaches us that "when our focus is on God, we stay in perfect peace." That is to say, we put reliable declarations in a prominent place. Integrity is valuable. It makes others question their loyalties. It reveals to you what is possible when faced with insurmountable obstacles. Integrity promotes unity in the faith and empowers you to be bold. It's what we can conclude from reading Psalm 119:165 as it emphasizes that there is ample peace for those who love God's teachings and instructions—they are unlikely to make missteps. Inner declarations must align with actions and the hope of the actions of others. Then they become outward declarations that support adjudications for better days.

Because we think before we declare, we can look at the Psalms and see a succinct statement that offers clarity concerning essential inner declarations: "I keep your precepts and testimonies, for all my ways are before you" (Psalm 119:168, ESV). Declarations are answers to what we observe. Inwardly, our hope is for the best outcome for our family and ourselves. To ensure that, it's best to view declarations as a part of your worldview that you are willing to share.

Chapter 3

Intentional Listening

Every remarkable accomplishment starts with a question. How do we erect this bridge over this river? Is it time to expand our business beyond the city limits? Is it worth staying through the tough times? The questions we present to the world first need internal examination. We must listen to a path well-traveled and a path less traveled. What I mean is this: Has anyone done what you are intending to do, and has there been a similar path you can study (or closely listen to) so you don't make the same pitfalls?

Questions:

- How many times do you need to repeat history before you listen?
- Is it true that wise counsel comes in the form of bystanders or entertainment?
- Are all my relationships necessary for reflection to get the most out of life?

Most of us, if we are honest, stand ready to respond without listening to the entire communication coming our way. Prejudging gets in the way of understanding so that the response has the appropriate intensity. For example, if you heard your child was misbehaving while at camp and you plan their punishment before you listen to the child, is that right? Does it matter if the people running the camp are good friends who deal with you honestly? What if you found out your child was with all the other kids smoking, and he was the one holding the camera, but he never smoked. Is he just as guilty, and does he require the same response you had before you heard the entire story? Some would answer yes, while others would say no. Listening to the child may reveal his position on smoking and why he decided to record the incident instead of participating.

The same resonates in a business relationship if we are consistent. Looking at a security monitor, it may seem that your colleague is taking money from the business. When you interact with the team, you find that something else is true. Did you intentionally watch the video and decide to turn in your colleague or remain suspicious for any other reasons? If so, your intentional listening may be askew.

Most of us listen with the mouth to respond versus listening with an ear to understand. Integrity is paramount if we want to take any relationship to the next level. Whether it be in business, intimate friendships, or family, we must remember to honor ourselves in such a way that we know what appears to be true is not always as it seems. In Psalm 141:1 (ESV), David writes, "O Lord, I call upon you; hasten to me! Give ear to my voice when I call to you!" This is a decree we all need. Understanding before we dissolve business ties or discipline a child adds to our integrity. Loving those around us means we listen with the intent to grow one another, not to tear down years of commitment. Life presents unforeseen trouble in so many ways, and as such, you will likely stumble. In fact, 2 Peter 1:9 informs us that we were cleaned up from going down the wrong path—that is to say, continually stumbling. Listening prevents us from undue stumbling.

Why do we forget that others may be on the wrong path or left the path of peace, righteousness, love, joy, and honor? The first step of intentional listening that promotes harmony is realizing any one of us can make a mistake or have a mistake interpreted the wrong way. It doesn't mean you ignore the mistake; it means there is a better way to respond that is helpful to everyone involved. When you repeat the same behaviors, especially those you can change easily, are you listening to wise counsel and the life you proclaim you desire?

To those who look for a lesson, they can find one in a movie, instructional video, books, and lectures, or a friendly conversation. "Doing wrong is like a joke to a fool, but wisdom is pleasure to a man of understanding" as Proverbs 10:23 (ESV) states. The pleasure of gaining wisdom overrides foolish behavior. The person planning to launch a new aircraft may be foolish to some; however, a mistake without proper investigation is the very act of a fool. A newly designed aircraft takes into consideration hours of intentional listening to provide the best chance at the desired outcome. Research is listening in the form of investigation. Friendly conversations are a solid foundation. You can add to that the lessons from people who study the task at hand.

A word of caution when you look for lessons from others: weigh them against someone who disagrees. Then look at it through the lens that serves the greatest loyalty any of us will ever experience.

Proverbs 12:15 (ESV) also adds, "The way of a fool is right in his own eyes, but a wise man listens to advice." The time it takes to listen to different teachers about a business venture or personal pursuit is the same as attending a lecture or watching a movie a few times a week. It takes a little discipline. The winner's attitude does not accept defeat without researching to see if there is a better way. Being surprised, in an instant, you are a single parent can be heart-wrenching. However, at this point in history, there are too many parents who deal with issues alone not to seek help. It doesn't always need to be a support group, though. For any surprising life change, some formal way of help may be the initial best choice. Is it wise to listen with an open heart to those who study conclusions from surprising life changes? A movie or a kind ear may do the trick for some situations. However, if your child—using the single parent example—is a different gender than you are, you may not know the best course of action when they become a teenager.

What does getting the most out of life look like to you? Is it having many treasured friendships or possessing material things? The kindest way to measure is to listen to what the end of life offers us in the present. If you believe "the person who dies with the biggest house and the most jewels wins," then you have your answer. Suppose you have all the material things you desire and still feel empty. Did you get the most out of life? Let's say you have many treasured friendships around the world. In any country you visit, you can stay at a friend's house for free indefinitely in any season of the year. Are you living your best life after achieving that lifestyle even if your income is not much more than the average person in your home country? What would they say about your lifestyle? Are you likely to get thumbs-up or thumbs-down to continue living that way?

Internal examination reveals fulfillment that comes through a thorough knowledge of oneself. To be clear, knowledge of yourself is not separate from knowing ultimately to whom you belong. Discovery of purpose fully exonerates any guilt toward the lack of action. How does that work? Actions are taken because we understand our purpose. James 2:18 explains that we show our faith through our corresponding actions. One is not exclusive from the other. Our purpose can be working as an architect, a hospital technician, or a carpet layer. We receive fulfillment because we intentionally listen to what is necessary to become fulfilled. Some are skilled laborers while others are magnificent caretakers. It doesn't mean one is less than the other. As you listen for greater clarity, you realize that many parts make up a society, and all of them are necessary (1 Corinthians 12:12-31).

In doing so, you reflect upon your life (or intentionally listen) to take note that we all are winners not by our position but by our value to one another. A relationship to food, work, friends, and the water supply or atmosphere first takes the form of listening to what you desire in a complete picture. What is most important to you? Yes, one relationship takes precedence over another by default or by emotional intelligence. No one can fix every complication in every relationship. However, everyone is responsible for intentionally listening to ferret out the best responses toward any complications. The hard-and-fast rules are: 1) listen with the intent to fully understand what words are being spoken, 2) listen to understand what words are left unsaid (that means, without judgment, listen to the character of the speaker), and finally 3) listen with the intent to love them no matter what.

It's obvious that intentional listening is the right thing to do. Are you talking while another speaks, consequently missing half the communication? Are you willing to test your response to the previous question? We know that listening to respond so we can offer wise counsel to others is the masterful way of listening. It is foolish not to seek the wisdom of a path well-traveled.

So how do you listen and keep privacy intact? Consider this: do not share with anyone you consider untrustworthy. It's okay to stop listening to one person's counsel and seek the counsel of another. Intentionally take time out to find someone who can deliver wisdom that is relevant to your life. Monitor your mentors and advisers. Ask them where they obtain their fruits of wisdom. Your relationships in business and otherwise will benefit as you take notes and journal your wisdom nuggets.

Chapter 4

Loving Hard

In a manner of speaking, "loving hard" often means extreme dedication to one another. The time it takes to love unconditionally certainly requires work and time, as many of you are aware. When emotion is the overriding effect of being in love, it can become nonsensical in its application. The promise of love is fulfillment. When love is not fulfilling, it's a detriment to you, those around you, and the greater community that experiences you "loving hard."

Questions:

- How did we get here?
- When do I get revenge?
- Can we examine love again?

Do you consider yourself a victim in love or a victim of love? Is it time to examine your response so that you understand how you landed in that space? Many understand that love gives us two basic things, hope and security (or assurance). When we are not assured, we panic and intend to destroy the person causing us to panic. Our minds are set for protection, and as such, we decide someone needs to suffer because we lack security.

Over time that ends up mixing with our hope for love to take care of us. The return on the investment of loving another, whether family or not, becomes a sore spot we must protect. So we no longer experience a kind love; we turn to "loving hard" because we intend to keep the relationships we started, come rain or shine. Emotionally, this is not sustainable. Physically, it is destructive. And to those around us, it is a case for retaliation from their perspective. Sometimes that retaliation is emotional and physical. For example, a child abuses someone at their school who reminds them of one of their parents in such an aggressive relationship.

Stop and ask yourself: Am I emotionally relevant to myself and those around me? Are my emotions beneficial to the life I intend to live? What we learn, we do. A carpenter learns from his father and then becomes one to feed his family. The other thing the young carpenter may learn is how to diffuse an argument between family members. Unfortunately, the young carpenter may learn from an older brother, instead of his father, to become the one who incites the argument. Thus we must all stop and ask ourselves whether we are emotionally intelligent. Not every aspect of living requires the highest emotional intelligence. Yet there is a need to show you are after the best for those you love and yourself.

To help, here are a few questions to ask yourself:

1. *If I were not my mother's (or father's) child, would they call me a fool for my actions in my relationships?* (Proverbs 10:1, ESV – A

wise son makes a glad father, but a foolish son is a sorrow to his mother.)
2. *Considering the person I admire the most, if they knew how I treated my spouse, would they give me a thumbs-up?* (Proverbs 26:12, ESV – Do you see a man who is wise in his own eyes? There is more hope for a fool than for him.)
3. *Why do I return to behavior for which those I respect the most have a negative opinion?* (Proverbs 27:17, ESV – Iron sharpens iron, and one man sharpens another)
4. *Am I able to speak to others about how to treat their girlfriend/ boyfriend and not experience inner turmoil?* (Proverbs 26:4, ESV – Answer not a fool according to his folly, lest you be like him yourself.)
5. *When I become angry, who does it serve?* (Ephesians 4:26, NIV – "In your anger do not sin": Do not let the sun go down while you are still angry.)

Too many people see anger as a virtue, and too many others regard it as a commodity. Some careers even consider aggression to be a prerequisite. That doesn't mean it's acceptable to display anger to settle a dispute. Anger is an asset to be deployed for the benefit of defense and learning. Consider what is written in Zephaniah 2:3, as it mentions seeking the Lord, staying humble, following the Lord's commands, and perhaps you will be protected from the day of the Lord's anger. It does mean anger is currently in use and will continue to be used. Is it beneficial, and is it used to exact revenge in your relationship? No, it's not love when anger is not useful. When you choose to punish an eighteen-month-old child, is it about furious anger or instruction?

Everyone you spend a significant amount of time with will disappoint you at some point—especially if you live with that person. Why is this a surprise after years upon years? Accept it as the basis of any old or new relationship. If you can claim such is not true, that is their first disappointment. The reason is that those people never let you see themselves in full. As one who carries such love and respect, it is necessary that you see they fall short too. How else can I offer my experience to you, in a career or relationship, if you never see me in some measure of fragility?

In my anger, do I accept what someone does to me? Some say this as they, in turn, punish themselves with some form of abuse. The abuse can be erratic behaviors, overeating, or using controlled substances. Revenge is never about getting even, especially when you turn on yourself. How often do you see someone say they feel as though things are settled after they get even? Many times the action of turning inward or outward to exact revenge becomes fear. The next stage of hurting others with vengeful actions means they or someone else may harm something or someone meaningful to you. Is that your goal? I mean to go back and forth, as long as it's sustainable, to keep exacting revenge. Do you accept that as your picture of a proper loving relationship, or is it necessary to change how we understand love?

The book of Ephesians teaches that we are to show humility and gentleness, with patience, bearing with one another in love. Also, we are to be eager to maintain the unity of the Spirit in the bond of peace (Ephesians 4:1-3, ESV). If we, in our closest relationships, are eager for zero interruptions in peaceful interactions, then we can contain our love. Reading 1 Corinthians 13:1-8, we see the definition of love. The first descriptive word used is that love is patient. If you understand that your spouse makes mistakes large and small, you must be patient first. Is it only okay for you to make mistakes when living in the same house for decades? I suggest that in most cultures their worldview would offer a resounding *no*. The reason is simple. It is justice.

Also, in 1 Corinthians, we read that love is not arrogant or rude. When you use the phrase "love hard," does it mean hurting someone when you don't have to? That is arrogant and rude. It's a way of saying you are above the other person for the moment, and it gives you permission to cause pain. Temporary as it may seem, it is not serving a healthy relationship. Rude behaviors are not seated in a life of harmony. When you are out in your community and see another person bump your car, you have the option to provide a harmonious response or the option to escalate the issue. If it is easy to push your buttons on such issues, I suggest a resolve that promotes harmony for yourself. When others push your buttons by being rude or bumping your car, it means they have more control over your emotional intelligence than you do. Certainly anyone can have an adverse response to a situation that gets out of hand. However, if it's what people think of you and how you think of yourself, consider changing loving hard to just love.

You may be saying, "That all sounds nice, but it's easier said than done." Anything we desire takes dedication, information, and action. We can get the information from several sources. I suggest a mentor who cares about you. The character of a mentor is fundamental. And it is noteworthy to mention that you need a mentor who cares about you as an individual. You can have a mentor for your career or your marriage. Both are necessary and generally easy to find; not all are good for you at the stage you're in, but starting is the best way to go forward. Paralysis through analysis stifles progress and ends in a mess.

One of the things I find consistent with those I advise is that they feel "You cannot dictate my response to what someone did to me." Such a response is basic and honest. We all have a right to our response emotionally. Our feelings are always trustworthy and genuine. On the other hand, our actions are not always trustworthy. Our response requires more thought. Living in a state of constant forgiveness is necessary to thrive in first-world countries with diverse cultures. Clashing one-on-one in a relationship is a challenge, and then mixing different ideologies and cultures is an additional challenge. A man clashes with a woman simply because they view the world differently. That very fact means it is necessary to be patient.

Leviticus 19:34 teaches that we are to treat a foreigner living among us as native-born. Why? Because that is what you would desire if you ever lived in an unfamiliar land. So having a new spouse move into your house is the wrong way to look at the situation. The foreigner is no longer a foreigner; they belong as much as you do. Wielding power that says otherwise is emotionally bankrupt and narcissistic. In effect, you're saying that you have the upper hand and you can make them leave whenever you desire. When you are in pain, your response belongs to you, and so do the level and frequency of your response. But that doesn't give you a pass for counterproductive actions. First Corinthians 10:23 says that all things may be allowed, but that doesn't mean they are beneficial.

It is only those who disregard others and their importance, who believe they can limit another's emotional responses and actions toward an issue. Do not let them. Guide their limitations by a proper worldview of love.

Chapter 5

Language—The Potency

What language do you desire from your partner in life, the person you told the world is "the one"? Whatever you say to them, is it okay for them to say it to you? Can they say it in the same manner, in the same places? How about toward others and with the same intent? Equity in business versus the family dynamic is not the same when we speak. Friends, family, and colleagues all have a hierarchy in their language, and it is potent.

Questions:

- How do I decide what words I will not use?
- How do I stop my progress by what I say in business and toward my family?
- Can we move forward?
- What difference does a culture within a culture make?

← Challenging Your Worldview →

What you proclaim to your friends, colleagues, and family is important to you. In the world, we set up different cultures through language. We accomplish this either through default, pain, or ignorance. In the book of Genesis, we see two brothers establishing hierarchy (Genesis 25:19-34). Jacob acquires his twin brother's birthright by giving him something to eat. This story exemplifies positioning oneself for immediate gain versus others for long-term gain. In the story, we discover that we can have different parents focusing on us as sons and daughters. Moreover, we can have vastly different temperaments within the same household, even among those born on the same date. The power of their language because of personality unwittingly has lasting effects.

In this hierarchy, we see that Jacob is prepared to obtain Esau's birthright because he immediately asks for it when Esau is hungry. Returning home after working in the field, Esau doesn't care about his birthright in the moment; he desires sustenance for his immediate satisfaction. Jacob takes advantage by asking for Esau's birthright. Patience in deception through your language is a dreadful way to handle family and colleagues. Calculated language to strike at a moment of weakness is not what you desire to be done to you or those you love.

Treating others with respect even when it is not returned requires being patient and forgiving. Don't merely listen to what you know is right; you must also do it (James 1:22). Being the most articulate is not the challenge of speaking clearly. More so, it is following your words with actions that shows who you are in this family or job. You want peace in your home? Then promote peace. If you desire that your coworkers act as a team, then you must both speak it and show it. When you see a group of individuals at work going in different directions, observe and offer some understanding, and then practice teamwork as you talk about it. Yes, it will take time for everyone to change. Some will try and fall away, and others may never change. The messenger is not the problem. You continue to show through your language the benefit of working as a team. What you may find is that when you are present, people will help you and not your other teammates. When this happens, you are starting a change for the better, and you can increase the potency of your language by simply asking one or two of them to accompany you as you help another. We know the results of never trying. If you change nothing, then nothing changes in your family or your job. Seek and use words to coincide with an intended outcome.

To accomplish a change in your business relationships and family, remember what is acceptable for you and your philosophy about language. Is it destructive? Then it is less likely you will achieve what is discussed in the former paragraph. Here in the third chapter of James, we see him express a contradiction in what we choose to say (James 3:10): "Out of the same mouth comes praise for God and then cursing towards your family." In that paraphrase, we understand that we have a choice to destroy or enlighten.

Here is the test, an understanding that you regard the following basic principle: there's a better way of speaking that holds me accountable. You can further examine that idea by asking if you are okay with your spiritual leader saying certain words. What about if they say those words to you or others in your home? Is it acceptable that your parents or grandparents say the identical words? What if you overheard your grandmother saying those same words to your senior spiritual leader? Is that acceptable? One last question: What if you heard your pastor say those words in prayer regarding you? Is it okay for you to use the same language? Redirecting your speech to a certain environment or a particular person means you are capable. "And the tongue is a fire, a world of unrighteousness. The tongue is set among our members, staining the whole body, setting on fire the entire course of life, and set on fire by hell" (James 3:6, ESV).

Let's suppose a directive came asking you and others to go to the grocery store and get milk, eggs, bread, tuna salad, water, salt and pepper, and bring back some apples from the neighbor's yard. Who is responsible for keeping track of the correspondence? Is it the person who gave the directive? The person receiving the message can carry blame too. The leader is ultimately responsible. Whoever's in charge of the situation is responsible for all directives to achieve the overall goal. Small bits of achieving the goal fall on the individual participants. When you have an opportunity to ensure that an overall plan works, you must communicate effectively because you are in charge. A child is still navigating understanding at a different level than his parents, who are in charge. Therefore, refine what you say so you can properly relate the message the child is receiving. Wait for feedback and remain ready to adjust.

Take note of Deborah, a judge, who discusses a directive with Barak about taking ten thousand men to fight Jabin's army. Barak acknowledges the Lord's directive and tells Deborah he is willing to go as long as she goes with him (Judges 4:4-10). His language speaks of understanding and acknowledging who is in charge. Further, there is an understanding about accomplishing the goal—taking out a general called Sisera from Jabin's army. The potency of the language displays unity and a clear objective. If you falter as a group of ten thousand, then you know individuals were not prepared properly, and you should never move unless you are sure.

That is how you stifle progress in your business. Too often leaders don't ensure the workers are properly prepared. Doing so means checking to see if the workers have enough food, not just seeing if they know the day's objective. It's okay to write down when lunch is going to happen. In a family setting, this makes it easier to manage others, especially when you have several different ages in your care. When leadership changes hands from parents to children, who themselves have grown children, it's a challenge to maintain a balance of respect. Language is even more substantial for balancing harmony in this scenario. First Thessalonians 1:2 (ESV) offers this: "We give thanks to God always for all of you, constantly mentioning you in our prayers." The balance is not only letting the others in the family know you pray for them; it's also important to let them hear that you are thankful for them. It gives them confidence as a member of the family to hear the family's leaders affirm them. Aging family members need relevance too no matter what their life's accomplishments may be. "A soothing tongue is a tree of life, but a perverse tongue crushes the spirit" (Proverbs 15:4, NIV).

Forceful language is not necessarily destructive. The potent language that allows you to move forward is inclusive even when you disagree. Potential is revealed to grow ourselves through our victories and defeats. Victories can be small, such as a young child carrying a watermelon to the house without smashing it on the sidewalk and receiving a pat on the back. Defeats can be destructive, such as burning the house down while falling asleep in the course of preparing a meal. In either case, the force of your language must promote harmony.

No matter what your position is in the family, offer clarity and hope. Both go together because hope is empty without direction. You set the potential for your language to become empty when you offer a form of hope with no attainable goals. To the hearer, it becomes rhetoric. Dwindling credibility is the result. After that, trust falls. To build trust, we can examine the book of Colossians as it says, "Let your speech always be gracious, seasoned with salt, so that you may know how you ought to answer each person" (Colossians 4:6, ESV). Smashing a watermelon on the street or burning down the house is upsetting, and yet they still need to move on.

Here is the challenge. When we're at home, it's one culture. Going to work, we find ourselves in another culture. Still another culture is interacting with our fellow countrymen and women. What is acceptable in one place is certainly not acceptable in another. We hold each in high regard based on having to belong. And if there is a problem at your job, it may be time for a change. Your charge is to be the light of the world (Matthew 5:16). That means you are to be an example to effect change in others around you. The greatest challenge is changing people outside your direct circle of influence. But this is not a reason to give up. You can simply be you, in constant refinement, and that affects every culture you touch.

The potency of your language in a culture derives from your response. When under attack, you don't have to reply with disrespect. An appropriate joke or misdirection works well. Other cultures recognize when you understand their attack. Also, they know when you are ignoring it for a favorable outcome. Yes, of course, some will be persistent and increase the attack. In no way am I saying you are to allow harm to come to what you are charged with protecting. However, we must understand this lesson: "Let no corrupting talk come out of your mouths, but only such as is good for building up, as fits the occasion, that it may give grace to those who hear" (Ephesians 4:29, ESV). "As it fits the occasion" is the remarkable part of that passage. Do you desire your children to hear you speak in anger toward a brother or sister who is out of hand? It's time to display your all-encompassing principles to others. Your maturity, morals, and values are being tested all at once. The potency of your language reveals where you are in that journey.

Your history may come from an unspeakable place. Some are from places where corruption and wickedness are prevalent. You are not destined to remain where you are from, and if you are, why consider growth? The lessons from a corrupt bloodline will never have a good place. And if it is good to you to proclaim lessons from your parents in every venue, then you should continue, even if it causes you to be removed from that venue. To move forward, you have to accept that there is room for error in what you learned from your culture. Many people are not moving forward because they accept their culture as the only way to live. Forgiveness has to work as you hear colleagues or people on the road of life exclaim disrespectful language. Otherwise, addressing each instance stops your life. Being an example of potent language means for you to "Let there be no filthiness nor foolish talk nor crude joking, which are out of place, but instead let there be thanksgiving" as a part of your way in building a better culture (Ephesians 5:4, ESV). A culture within a culture can revive the culture's true value. Proverbs adds to this saying, "For lack of wood the fire goes out, and where there is no whisperer, quarreling ceases" (Proverbs 26:20, ESV).

Try doing this the next time you say something off-putting to someone: write down how it would make you feel if the same person said it to you. Next, write down as many reasons as you can think of as to why they cannot or will not say the same to you. We must remember that "…no human being can tame the tongue. It is restless evil, full of deadly poison" (James 3:8, ESV). Surrender your language to the potential we all have in love.

Chapter 6

Leading with the Arrogance of Ignorance

In today's information age, it's challenging to know what to believe. There are so many outlets and venues that teach different topics relevant to our lives. Leading a family or taking the helm of a business department means there will be obstacles to overcome. Which one do you prefer—the arrogance of being right or the humility of being righteous? The best family or business outcomes are always strategic. Critically thinking through what to believe and seeking wisdom wins battles before you get into the trenches. Therefore, the best platform from which to springboard considers: *What does victory look like?*

Questions:

- Do I have a responsibility to seek wisdom?
- How do I know if I am leading a family with confidence?
- What does leading a family astray mean?

If you examine Proverbs, you see a passage that promotes obtaining wisdom and understanding (Proverbs 4:7). As such, you have a responsibility to obtain information. Is the information meant to prove you are right, or is it to be humble because your character reflects righteousness? The correct application of that information is understanding. When you know how to travel from your house to work efficiently, you do it. Better yet, when you know the best way to travel for your family—considering time, safety, and monetary limitations—you apply it. The same goes for your active participation in getting information.

Many places have concrete information that is researched and reviewed by either peers of the respective conclusions or naysayers. How do you decide? First, your morality clause is foundational. Do you have a basis from which to examine how you lead? To lead others, you need to accept that there are limitations, or shall we say guardrails. There is a price to be paid when you and the business are in trouble. It's a challenge to know which direction to go in when your values are not in check. Use the guardrails to help you navigate the information you must apply to move forward.

For example, when your business needs to expand to stay relevant in the community, you may have two simple options: open a business across town or build a bigger location near your current location. Depending on the product or services, having two locations may mean you lose the same level of service. The other option is to expand in the same location and train others so that you can ensure when you do decide to have another location, it reflects the values of the primary business model wholeheartedly. Either option may look appealing. However, when you seek wisdom, from a mentor and others, you may find an even better solution that fits the current trends for your product. Yes, a mentor is a guardrail.

In a family, a leader has much more responsibility to others in a service capacity. A business leader too must serve. However, family members need to be dressed, bathed, fed, and often taken to different locations. Sometimes you, as the leader, will need help from family members in the same ways. What did you lead them to understand about keeping a family unit viable in difficult times? Is the answer "fend for yourselves at all cost?" It's certainly not the most humble and inclusive way to promote the family. In 1 Timothy 5:8 (ESV) we read, "But if anyone does not provide for his relatives, and especially members of his household, he has denied the faith and is worse than an unbeliever."

From a child's perspective, is it easy to follow a thief, an adulterer, or a liar? As a child watches they will obtain some form of morality. It may be from school or friends; however, we apply what we understand as we grow. The leader's responsibility is to see if the family members understand that what is acceptable in the home is also acceptable in society. The only basis for this is seeking the necessary wisdom to navigate the world with an unshakeable level of morality. Moreover, it means what you profess in words must be shown in actions (Titus 1:16).

The place a business or family leader starts is no excuse for staying the same year after year. In an age where information is at your fingertips or easily accessible at a library, you can start reading and listening to information right now. You can document your reasoning and conclusions in a journal. Many who use a journal know that a journal only needs to make sense to you. Oftentimes people fear others reading their journal. Whatever you hear or read can be written in your journal in the form of a positive that only you understand. A journal doesn't have to be a book where you confess all your innermost thoughts. Taking responsibility as a leader includes measuring the growth of others, but foremost it's measuring the growth of yourself. Years later, when reviewing your journal, you will see what you accepted into your life as viable to lead others.

A family is a UNIT: Undeniably Needing Individuals Together. Each person within a UNIT has concerns, fears, expectations, physicality, revelations, beliefs, dreams, goals, and so forth. A leader should cultivate a short-term and long-term plan of fulfillment for these various aspects of the UNIT. Do this in the morning before everyone is up, or late at night. Respectfully speak of your family in prayer. Humility is a trustworthy virtue toward peace in a home. As a leader who desires to model correct behaviors in different situations, practice speaking in terms that build the family members up. "But encourage one another daily, as long as it is called 'Today,' so that none of you may be hardened by sin's deceitfulness" (Hebrews 3:13, NIV). Affirming your family to yourself and God makes it easier to speak to them without malice. Yes, in a UNIT there will be individuals who forget their need for togetherness and will come against your language. This is where discipline and expectations are necessary.

Leading with the arrogance of ignorance also entails believing that a family does not need maturing. Adults in the family need guidance just like the children. Let me be clear: an adult is never to be corrected or trained. Guidance and mentorship are what need to take place. That discussion takes more mentorship than will be discussed in this book. What I am writing about is proper behavior and discussions when reconciliation is of the utmost importance to move forward. When two people who decide to lead the family chastise one another openly or in private, the answers have already been written. Because of the hardness of your heart, you will walk toward a divorce (Matthew 19:8). Humility is being able to let the leader lead.

Facing a financial strain may be problematic. And the dad in the family states it is his responsibility to provide for the family. If that is the decision, it's okay. That doesn't mean the dad is better at finances than the twenty-one-year-old niece who's been living with the family for ten years and understands how to navigate financial situations better. Supporting the niece is the best way to lead the family. The leader will bolster confidence in everyone so that their talents are viewed as worthy and necessary to the UNIT.

Another good way to affirm, not only through words but also through actions, is allowing younger members opportunities to make decisions. Dinner is an easy way to have younger children take responsibility for leading the family. Depending on their age, allow them to make a meal plan. Help them remember all the people in the family—like grandma, who may have diabetes, or a son who had a birth complication requiring a special diet. As they get older, the next step is having them prepare the meal and cook it. For the older child, it may be time to plan the meals financially and possibly decide which restaurants to go to considering every family member's needs. Too often families focus on chores as a means of responsibility, yet it doesn't bolster confidence as much as planning and leading for the UNIT.

The environment we can control is crucial because our children will be in environments we cannot control. No one institution or organization is perfect. Planning prevents improper decisions outside the home life. In business, we consider the mission and value statements as the intended direction of the company. A UNIT needs a mission and value statement too. Unfortunately, too many leaders within an organization fail to live up to the expectations, and sometimes their deeds are unbearable. The results are that the leaders are replaced, and often the culture remains the same if a mentee (or a child) from the previous leader takes over. This means the organization is now led by the same unethical deeds. What's necessary to understand is what you will do as someone who's in charge of the UNIT or business. Will you follow your mentor, the proposed mission and value statements, or forge a path of constant refinement?

You may stay around and try to change the atmosphere, if plausible. The other option is to vacate so that you maintain some level of care toward your values. Maturity without conviction is empty. James 2:26 says, "...faith without works is dead." When you follow a leader who does not exemplify maturity nor seek wisdom, it may be time to depart as you may become like those around you (Proverbs 22:24-25).

For the family, a leader must show how to pray, how to greet others, and how to reflect. Allow the children to pray, and add to your journal the growth you see in them from age three to fifteen. It will be a reflection of your leadership. Further, this will give you a chance to apply a different technique as you lead that you've obtained from the time of their younger age until now. As the children watch you, as the leader(s), they learn how to grow and what to accept as viable teaching. Therefore, allow your children to see you and your spouse teach one another. It is not abdicating position or authority. It's promoting value in position and authority. First Peter 3:7 (ESV) teaches, "Likewise, husbands, live with your wives in an understanding way, showing honor to the woman as the weaker vessel, since they are heirs with you of the grace of life, so that your prayers may not be hindered." Whatever you consider the weakness of your spouse, it is your responsibility to value what they bring to the UNIT and allow it to flourish. The example of the adults (including grandparents) sets the stage for what a child will need to fight through to obtain victory in life.

Where are you? Do you have conversations with your younger children and your older children too? It can be a challenge to manage children of different ages, especially if you're naturally drawn to a certain age. Some people prefer toddlers and others prefer teenagers. In the family, it's necessary to remember you never stop. A momentary pause may be needed to maintain a level head. This does not mean you can forget you are the leader in the family.

That may seem obvious; however, I'm describing balance. When a child is learning from their parents, it's necessary for them to see that the parents need time to reflect and grow. They need to understand that the world is not just filled with their expectations. You are leading them somewhere, and they need to realize the same. Never informing them of where they're going leads them astray. It's easier to have people follow when they can picture the goals and outcomes that benefit their world. For a family, it means making a plan that offers peace and harmony even in tough times. It means laying out how you will discipline the children.

For example, tell your ten-year-old boy that when you return home, if the dishwasher is not empty, he cannot participate in online gaming. When he realizes the two go together, no matter what, he's likely to reconcile a choice that fits his interest. A child will reflect on a choice that allows them to understand that their actions (or inactions) lead them somewhere.

Chapter 7

Is Now Like Then—
Can I Count on You?

Up until now, you noticed your patterns don't change even when you ask others for advice. A lot of us ignore wisdom from people we celebrate as great thinkers. Sometimes we even tell others to ask for advice from those we admire. Still, we don't follow it. The people around us desire and need to know if we are receiving wisdom and how it will change us. And, if it's rich enough insight to offer others, why are you cavalier toward the messenger or the offering of knowledge? Wisdom is not just for what is coming.

Questions:

- How do I know if it is time for me to change?
- Why should I want to trust you?
- Forgiveness—is it real?

When it rains, an umbrella may bend. Yet you count on it and bring it with you on a rainy day. You know that you too may bend in a storm, and the person who brought you with them is counting on you. They know you may bend; however, they have you present because they believe you can deal with the storm. Wisdom to deal with any storm is not always easy in its application. The challenge for many of us is to accept the wisdom as applicable. That means going forward with the pain of making different choices.

In Joshua 3:1-4, the officials tell the Israelites to follow a familiar path and yet keep their distance from the Ark of the Covenant. Here we see a group of people given the wisdom to follow. Examining the passage, you see a few pieces of wisdom you can apply—notably to keep your distance from something you may desire to touch or experience.

The experience of something interesting to you is always something to enjoy. How can it not be? Does your past dictate your future? Is this true, even now, with new information that promotes your well-being? Moreover, does it promote what you profess as a proper and healthy life? To many of us, life is a journey of reconciliation. It also needs to be a life of promise. We reconcile to be content. However, in that, we produce an acceptable life to Christ (1 Timothy 6:6).

How is it possible for you to desire to change and be content at the same time? Begin each day with a purpose. Yes, there will be obstacles. Just as the officials informed the Israelites crossing the Jordan, it will be a time to see the path, and it will be a familiar path. When you seek information, take notes and even journal because you may need this information in the not-too-distant future. You may also need it years from now to instruct your children. Everything you get is not for you. It's for you to give. That promise for every day makes it possible to change directions. Intentionally get wisdom so that you can pass it along.

Think about the ramifications of a culture that ignores this simple principle. The opportunity for growth within that collection of people is stifled by previous generations. When you act upon the idea that it's better to give than to receive, it means you have something to give. No one can change without dealing with the fact they don't have something of equitable power that offers change to someone else. The time to do that is now.

Old opinions of who you were will consistently become a paradoxical moment for you. Many will draw you back by compelling words, invitations, and mockery. The time to stand strong is during these moments. Remember to ask yourself, "Is today intentionally a changing day or not?" Listen carefully to those who present those options to you. Understand that they are not asking you to return to an old life. They are presenting you with an opportunity to show strength in how you move forward. Moreover, they're saying they are hungry for change themselves. Take it as courage that the wisdom you are seeking is working. Therefore, you don't need to touch what is unacceptable to you now.

In a close relationship, such as with a spouse or longtime friend, it's much harder to change. Trusting a person with intimacy is a huge part of every chapter of your existence. We all expect betrayal at any moment. That itself makes you cautious about the people you trust. A fallen person is only trustworthy when their worldview is being refined. Part of changing outwardly is working with people who are close to you. If the very next day, without warning, you tell your spouse that you're going jogging every morning, it may at first be met with glee. Next, uncertainty and questions are likely to follow. Remember, in a close relationship, what the other expects is a part of trust. Combining two lives as close friends or in marriage, it's necessary to communicate changes to the other's lifestyle.

Over a period of years, no one is likely to keep focusing on what can be when they don't see consistent incremental change. Hope is not evidence. It's a placeholder for what is to come. Its relevance comes because others see you collecting the tools for the change. In terms of a relationship where trust is broken, you must put into practice reasons to expect a different outcome than previous experiences. Confidence in your spouse is like what we extend to people in a restaurant: we expect reasonable people to do humane things. Unfortunately, after we experience something profoundly different, we are not likely to return for such a dining experience.

Considering that no two people are exactly alike, we must acknowledge that a patient journey lies before us in life. When you obtain a new friend, be aware that something you will not like about them is likely to appear. Personality quirks, physical attributes, or other people in their life can cause some distance between you two. Whenever you realize this, be aware that they are experiencing the same regarding you. Once you solidify the relationship in business, friendship, or marriage you are in effect acknowledging their oddities as acceptable. Keep this in mind, because even if you can't say it directly to them, and they aren't comfortable expressing it to you, it's acceptable to both of you. Your view of the world and your life's plan says, in all the people you have experienced thus far, that you are willing to join your journey with this person (or people). It's advisable to ask where a person gets their information about how to conduct business and love—then take time to review that way of seeing the world. The results will solidify trust of oneself and those you invite along on your journey.

Forgiveness takes time and consistency to settle in so that others have an appropriate response. Whether it's forgiving yourself or another, we can offer words and encouragement; however, it's a challenge to act differently. With that, words are necessary, and the accompanying tasks are more substantial. In a business relationship, it may be necessary to break legal ties or resign from the position. Two people going in opposing directions is difficult enough when there is a need for forgiveness. A person and an organization that need reconciliation face a tremendous task. Loving those in the organization from afar is likely the better choice. Although, if willing to do the work, it's possible to reconcile, which means follow-through.

A business relationship holds certain confidence unlike that with family members. It is well to express a different side of yourself. Many of you hold back, while some go for it, and whatever happens is okay. Putting a part of your personality or reputation on the line as a worker means a lot to maintain a healthy mindset. Diverse strengths arise to maintain a career that is not suitable for where you are regarding your worldview. Understand that where you are is an assignment to obtain wisdom to pass to others. All points of light regarding wisdom are not grand. However, when you pass the information along to another, it can mean a world of difference.

To maintain reverence toward wisdom:

1. *Uphold your integrity even when it hurts your reputation.* (Proverbs 19:1, ESV: "Better is a poor person who walks in his integrity than one who is crooked in speech and is a fool.")
2. *Find a healthy way to deal with the fact that others will always have an opinion of you.* (Proverbs 4:24, NLT: "Avoid all perverse talk; stay away from corrupt speech.")
3. *I count on you to be you.* (Matthew 5:37, ESV: "Let what you say be simply 'Yes' or 'No'; anything more than this comes from evil.")

You have to be consistent with the new character that says, "Now is not like then." Are you a member of the UNIT that we can rely upon? Can you count on yourself, not for perfection, but enough to be considered reliable? That is when personal forgiveness is real. Knowing you are in concert with the practices of Jesus, the Savior, as the leader of your worldview allows you to forgive. If you use a different worldview, does it allow for sincere reconciliation? Unless you are willing to cease-fire toward those who did you wrong, you are struggling with forgiveness.

Understand that at times you will remember what was done to you and what you can do about it. Redirect those thoughts and filter them through this passage: "For with the judgment you pronounce you will be judged, and with the measure you use it will be measured to you" (Matthew 7:2, ESV).

In a world of imperfect people, much will be done to you that is hard to forgive. Love reconciles to itself that people fall short, and that affects the people around them. When you are willing to teach others in love, which provides opportunities for violence, you realize your worldview is being perfected.

Chapter 8

The People Around You

As the world becomes more globally interconnected through social media and business, it's easier to interact with people with different worldviews. The hope is that those connections, even if started in person, remain authentic. Of course, if only online—though unlikely—one hopes they are just as authentic. It's harder to interact with a person and determine their worldview when there are many barriers between you.

Questions:

- What barriers should I expect?
- Why is their problem my problem too?
- Am I to accept their worldview?

Finding common ground is a mandate of exemplary living. If only you could isolate yourself, the problems of the world would be solved for you, right? Not so fast. Only a few of us understand enough science and agriculture to live totally off the grid. Many of us realize we need others to thrive. Moreover, we want to thrive alongside friends and family, and part of living a satisfying life is sharing. It is hoped that you ask yourself, "What do I need to understand in this life with my family and business colleagues?"

The answer resembles acceptance of people as just that, people. Everyone has room to become a better citizen of humanity. You are to act as a benefit to them and yourself. What benefit do you see in working only in isolation toward your goals? No goal is at its best in isolation. That is the relationship mandate that includes those around you.

The prospect of benefiting from another person should excite you. No team member holds onto information about a game they play when you have insight into winning. Your desire is for the team to win. If you are a part of that team, you must add to the team's wisdom. The same goes for a UNIT or business. Are you the barrier by simply not providing information?

Yes, of course, many times the team cannot handle what you want to say or how you say it. Find an alternate way to express yourself. Although it may sound simple, write it in a text message or on paper. If on paper, rehearse it and say it to one or two people to give a critique, and then refine what you want to say. In the moment, you may not have time during a game when the buzzer is about to sound. However, preparation is the key in more stressful times. A fellow team member may be able to express what you want to say better. That's the reason you need to recognize how people view and understand you. It's a challenge to accept that others don't apply the same compliments that you do toward yourself.

Listening is a skill that many would say others need to improve. But far too many of us don't accept that we are to listen with the intent to change our reactions. Loving you means taking note of how you want to be loved. For example, some people don't like public displays of affection, while others demand it. To remove the barrier, you must converse and compromise without reservation. When you compromise with reservations you are creating more barriers. Accepting the compromise means accepting the new way of life. It does take time to work through the challenges of different values and philosophies. Eventually, you and the others should be excited about the new direction. Take that as a part of what makes living worth it.

Another barrier you may not expect is found in the book of Hosea. In the second chapter, we see a passage concerning his wife: "For their mother has played the whore; she who conceived them [her children] has acted shamefully. For she said, 'I will go after my lovers, who give me my bread and my water, my wool and my flax, my oil and my drink'" (Hosea 2:5, ESV). Her way of thinking is troubling, and she misunderstands; however, being connected means you deal with another's worldview as it is currently. It is what Christ did for us. Our commitment to God is not in contrast with His salvation. It is in concert. Connecting your life to another person's journey means you are accepting the lesser-known qualities and faults they possess. You need this information; otherwise you will work heartily toward a different goal. Rerouting your actions to benefit everyone involved takes more patience than we can imagine, especially when dealing with someone like Hosea's wife.

No matter how you arrived in the life of a business colleague or family member, dedication is part of the commitment. Many believe commitment means "until"—that is to say, until you do something unbearable; then I'm leaving. Dedication means even if you or I have to leave, I am willing to help you. "...I say to you, Love your enemies and pray for those who persecute you" (Matthew 5:44, ESV). Yes, a business colleague may be easier to leave than someone whom you spent years combining lives with. Your worldview is acceptance of certain philosophies and practices as you act. It shows what you expect from yourself toward others. Keep in mind that forgiveness takes down many barriers. And family members will need continual forgiveness, as you do. Forgiving is not forgetting. It is removing a barrier so that your journey is noteworthy.

Committing to Hosea's wife may be easy for one man, and for another it could be the deal-breaker. Hoping one day they will realize you are the better choice is not how you want to live. But their problem is your problem when you accept that their journey, although connected, even if temporary, is theirs to live. That is a challenge for any of us to accept. No one wants to live in the same house, in marriage, and be alone. This is especially true if the wife has the same way of thinking as Hosea's. It is proper to question the basis of their journey and their worldview because it can be too askew.

Being open enough to accept that your housemates—children, grandchildren, or younger siblings—experience life differently than you is crucial to being at peace in your life. Your language must reflect bringing peace to a situation versus being a rabble-rouser. A cord made up of three strands is not easily broken, to paraphrase Ecclesiastes 4:12. Knowing who is around you and their view of how to handle difficult situations will allow your home to be safe. The time to find out your grandfather hates defending his home and would rather flee is not when the intruder is at the door.

You cannot force a business partner or loved one to accept your worldview in a spare moment. It takes a conversation about the difficult things in life. One simple way is to discuss what they love to read or their favorite shows. Just because someone accepts it in a book as a way to go about life does not mean they accept it in reality. Here is an example of a common question within relationships: Is it better for a husband to just do the dishes after a meal, or is it better for him to ask for permission? Some may say, "He should just do the dishes." However, take into consideration where you live and the others in the house. Some are territorial and would consider it an insult that you touched certain dishes, even in your home.

To promote a happy home, remember that a suggestion can be a question, and a question can be a suggestion. The important thing is to communicate with clarity and wait for an affirming response. Keep in mind that a "yes" today may change tomorrow. The reason is that as others learn your patterns, they may no longer have the same worldview about your participation. So listen for the answers for now and in the future—intentional listening. All the time that is happening, you are promoting a simple concept of clarity through being consistent in your worldview of a happy home or work life. That's the security we all desire.

Now, what happens when those I've chosen to work with daily, either in business or at home, have a view of things that is foreign to me? The complete picture to accepting another's worldview is patience. God offers grace. No two people work together without first finding some common ground. Of course, a child's common ground is easy to find. And, remarkably, that is the place to find common ground for adults. What things are common to us all? In 1 Corinthians 10:13 we find that "no temptation takes over you that is not common to us all people…." That's a good place to start. Offer up a yes as there are so many positives to experience, such as food, gardening, science, travel destinations, etc. We all want some form of interaction with the world around us. Utilize that to break the ice to find some commonality.

Start there and grow your understanding so that working together is not painful for you or them. No one will relinquish their worldview so readily to another, even if they trust you. That is not the goal, at least not initially. The goal is breaking barriers so that coherent and authentic relationships can be formed. The older we become the less likely we are to change our worldview unless something drastic happens. What we know is that accepting another's worldview is less about us changing them and more about them having the most honest and complete expression in their life. "Him we proclaim, warning everyone and teaching everyone with all wisdom, that we may present everyone mature in Christ" (Colossians 1:28, ESV).

Chapter 9

Money's Purpose

Most people see money as a means to an end—often as a transaction to obtain what they want or need. The challenge is to realize the people in your life need you to manage your money properly. To be a good steward of money, you must understand its service characteristic and lead by showing others. A gift is only as big as the giver's reason and the recipient's understanding of the reason. The attraction of the gift, or the giver, can be positive or negative as a result.

Questions:

- Is it immoral to want money?
- How do I view financial security?
- Why is wealth measured by the world and the kingdom of God?

To ensure clarity in our discussion, being wealthy is different from being rich. For a person to be wealthy, they must bring in more than enough money to live in their respective culture, whether through active or passive income. In other words, a job is not required for them to have a consistent paycheck. Many people only believe you are wealthy after you hit a certain monetary number. Challenging that perspective, we can look at a third-world country versus the many retirees in North America. A person suffering from an oppressive regime in a third-world country would likely consider what a lot of retirees earn in North America as extreme wealth.

Rich people have more than enough; however, they must continue to work to maintain a certain income. Many of them can indeed retire on less than they earn and move to a wealthy financial picture. Either way, the main point is that when you bring in the money it is purposeful beyond what you may initially believe.

So is it wicked to want lots of money? To answer that question, I would ask first: What are you going to do with the money? Is it to show off or to have basic things in life? Desires can corrupt the heart and take you away from a solid purpose. First Timothy 6:9-10 (ESV) tells us, "But those who desire to be rich fall into temptation, into a snare, into many senseless and harmful desires that plunge people into ruin and destruction. For the love of money is a root of all kinds of evils. It is through this craving that some have wandered away from the faith and pierced themselves with many pangs."

Over and above your heart's desires, what can you obtain? Is the answer better security, another boat, or even the purchase of an island? Then what? Loving others means trusting yourself to do right by them whenever possible. Too often family, advisers, and friends teach you to share but leave out the reason. Taking care of others is taking care of yourself. Yes, some will return selflessness with selfishness, and that is painful when you work hard and give. The heart's picture likely contains joy to share what you purchase with others. When you obtain a new level of income, ask yourself what it means for those you love—even those you do not know personally.

To those who have never experienced poverty, financial security looks different. Many times the question is asked of people of means, "How much is a gallon of milk or a loaf of bread?" A lot of times the poor are unaware too. There are a few different reasons for this concerning both groups of people.

The financially secure, for the most part, never need to consider the amount of money they spend on basic food items. It depends on their lifestyle. Those struggling with finances may be unaware because they don't understand money.

Of course, this is not true of all people struggling with finances. Too many of them never expect to go into a grocery store with enough money to shop. Some go after one or two items to make it through the day. Interacting with either of them, you realize they view financial security as either something not worth mentioning or irrelevant to them because of the situation in which they find themselves.

The lesson is that both know they need security. After spending a great deal of your life struggling or in poverty, while seeing others flourish, it's normal to want a better existence. Some people with more than enough money view struggling as getting to the next level of wealth. Some do it for a redeemable purpose, and others do it for selfish reasons. Accept that existence with or without money must have relevance. Security is not only for our earthly mission; it is for the ever-after too. When speaking to business partners or your spouse, ask, "What is the purpose of financial success?"

In business, it may be to expand so that you can be charitable and give generously, as Romans 12:8 explains. In a relationship, it's to secure your family for now and in the future so that basic things are never a problem and the family can focus on faith. Feed them first, then teach them the principle we find in James 2:16 (ESV), "And one of you says to them, 'Go in peace, be warmed and filled,' without giving them the things needed for the body, what good is that?" Within your family, concern yourself with that concept. The ultimate in security is when a soul feels comfortable enough to explore the Word of God without regard for the body's basic needs.

Remember your Creator who provides a way for you to obtain enough money to do the work set forth by Him through you (Deuteronomy 8:18). You may believe it's only reciprocal to those who participate. You are participating even if you're unaware of the mandate of sowing and reaping. Speak to your spouse about what they would like to give away when the children are out of the house. It will reveal how they see the possessions you collectively have obtained. It will also reveal if they relate those possessions to God's purpose. Will the answer for you contain any charitable giving or transactional interactions? For example, does the person receiving owe you anything? Do they owe you an explanation concerning what they will do with your gift? Offer an opportunity as you give, not a deal.

A covenant with the Creator is reciprocal. In the singular, God is not separate from wealth and worship, so as you honor the kingdom with the wealth you have, it returns to you (Deuteronomy 26:10-11). God measures your ability to understand. In a basic sense, you do something with the ability to understand. Eve ate the forbidden fruit because of her deception in understanding (Genesis 3:1).

You either give in the form of food, clothing, or teaching or keep those things to yourself. How do you know if you are interacting with God in the sense of honor? Consider this text from Matthew 6:21 (ESV) as it says, "For where your treasure is, there your heart will be also." Time, money, affection, protection, and dreams all play a role in what you treasure. When examined, what will your treasures reveal about you?

Taking a closer look at time, money, affection, protection, and dreams, we see a link to the four types of love. Starting with *phileo*, brotherly love, we understand that we spend money and time with friends and express our dreams. Next, protective love, or *storgé*, is taking care of your family and often is the reason you go after money or take overtime shifts when available. Following that is erotic love, or *eros*, which is romantic and contains dreams and affection toward your spouse. Finally, we have *agape*, which combines them all in proper context because it is godly love. Without the ability to love friends and family properly, those interactions are misaligned. The result is treasures misspent.

Now, financial success doesn't look the same for everyone. Success in Christianity doesn't look the same either. Culture may teach that money reveals success. It does not. The reason we correlate the two in certain circles is that we want to show our love for God and that God loves us. You may forget that God's love for you may entail keeping financial success away from you. Even after accepting salvation, you may not be ready. Made in the image of God, your sovereignty is realizing His purpose over and above what you can fathom. Money is not a means to an end; rather, it's about obtaining the means to effect the end. Ecclesiastes 9:11 (ESV) teaches, "Again I saw that under the sun the race is not to the swift, nor the battle to the strong, nor bread to the wise, nor riches to the intelligent, nor favor to those with knowledge, but time and chance happen to them all." A chance to have an abundance of money for you means the opportunity to effect a better end for more people, quicker.

In so much as we understand that concept, we must accept being content. "But godliness with contentment is great gain, for we brought nothing into the world, and we cannot take anything out of the world," as it says in 1 Timothy 6:6-7 (ESV). The challenge for a couple is to decide how to make money together and be content with where you are in life's journey. Realizing the ebb and flow of life may mean some setbacks concerning money. Prepare for them as you do for anything else. How will you divide the duties of making, managing, and growing your money to establish God's work through you?

A big house needs a purpose better than showing it off to friends and colleagues.

Host events and help the community, or use it as a place of refuge so others can get on their feet. The home is also a place to relax or protect others as plans go forth to do God's work.

A small home is adequate for those who don't spend much time in it. For example, suppose you work a lot out of town or do missionary work. For what reason do you have a big home? Of course, if you have a family to house, it makes sense that the house is comparable. In either case, be content and realize the reason for the blessing of your domicile.

By grace you can turn away from stealing God's talents for selfish gain. "Let the thief no longer steal, but rather let him labor, doing honest work with his own hands, so that he may have something to share with anyone in need," as we are reminded in Ephesians 4:28 (ESV). You don't want to live a life of offense toward others as your worldview does not see that as acceptable, does it? So all of us are not to offend neighbors by disrespecting them with wealth or riches. We find further understanding in 1 John 3:17 (ESV), "But if anyone has the world's goods and sees his brother in need, yet closes his heart against him, how does God's love abide in him?" Moreover, God finds it offensive to harass and dominate the less financially fortunate (Proverbs 14:31). You can redirect how you see the treasures you have, big or small, by aligning them with agape love, and that is good news.

Chapter 10

Picture Yourself as Offended

It is offensive to equate the reflection of something to that of the original's power. Is your shadow the same as you? Those who desire worship are not acknowledging the power of the original Creator. To receive offense underscores a certain amount of power from the offender. As such, consider the offense and pain you can dole out and see if you know your limits. Next, ponder what allows any of us to be offended beyond repair. A family's purpose is to bolster you, and that is something you replicate in love, not offense.

Questions:

- What do *you* get to decide regarding *my* power to offend?
- How can I be responsible?
- Can I offend God?

Sitting alone and afraid in an interrogation room is a girl, age fifteen. She portrays herself as tough by her dress and what she displays on her body. On the streets, she expects no one will come at her offensively. In fact, she remains ready to destroy you with her abhorrent language. A calm female police captain enters the room, never moving her eyes away from the young suspect. She walks closer and leans into the girl, who unleashes the most violent language the policewoman can imagine. After a long rant, still handcuffed, the girl pauses to see what the judgment will be.

Unfazed, the police captain asks her a simple question: "What about any of what you just said do you think I receive as offensive or haven't heard—or been called—before?" Taking a beat, the young girl realizes she didn't make a mark on the police officer. Quickly, the youngster tries another tactic and goes for tears. She observes that the older woman is still not fazed.

Too often we believe "my offense is yours" and vice versa. We forget that someone older or younger or in a different culture may have life experiences to a degree much greater than we can imagine. What we see in front of us is not always as it appears. We make observations through our perspective. In Acts 2, we see an explanation concerning speaking in different languages after receiving a gift. The offenders mock them saying, "They are filled with wine."

You can decide based on personal experience and observation what is happening to you. Because coworkers and family are not seeing things from your perspective doesn't mean they are not offended or have the right to be offended. Too many of us believe that because we are not offended, you shouldn't be either. Also, many hold the belief that they can decide if you are offended. That is a form of self-worship or idolatry. Your feelings are always valid. It does not mean they are always healthy (to you or the larger human community). So who gets to decide whether your feelings are healthy? That's where your worldview comes into play.

Further, understand you don't get to decide the level of offense. As a person worth the same as any other, the intensity of offense is up to you as the offended. As much as that is true, the level of response is up to you as well. When a person offends someone and then says to them, "It was not that hurtful," they are in effect telling you they dictate your feelings. That's another offense, not only to them but also to you, the offender, as it takes the form of idolatry.

Responsibility is up to you. Romans 12:18 (NIV) teaches, "If possible, so far as it depends on you, live at peace with everyone." Why is it your life choice to offend? Pain, regret, or fear that causes you to offend is a mark of unresolved issues. Yes, the one receiving the offense gets to choose if they are not offended. However, you get to choose peace or chaos, offense or harmony. "Let us therefore make every effort to do what leads to peace and to mutual edification," Romans 14:19 (NIV) tells us.

Being proactive in making better choices takes time and work. You can write down your prayers concerning your family. Either short or long, it gives you a perspective regarding your housemates. Over time, review what you write and update the language to reflect a healthier view. In addition, add what you appreciate about each family member and what they bring to your family.

Reducing offense also means seeing others as significant. So as your journal contains how you see them, it's necessary to add what you desire for the future too. What is your goal for your fifteen-year-old versus when they were five? Do you have goals for your spouse that remain unshared? Are they expecting things from you that only surface during a disagreement? The intensity of feeling upset and resentful is magnified when your housemates are unaware of your belief in their future.

At first it may seem foreign to use helpful language, especially if that's not how you usually relate. Yes, expect family members to be surprised or even to reject it. Moving forward, consistency is what matters. This relies on your actions and changing your beliefs toward offensive behavior. The healing process is not an overnight fix. In Ephesians, we find this reason to pause and reflect on our actions: "'In your anger do not sin': Do not let the sun go down while you are still angry" (Ephesians 4:26, NIV). Are your children and spouse subject to the sin in your anger? Do they fit into the healthy version of your worldview of a family?

Romans 14:17 (ESV) provides this view, "For the kingdom of God is not a matter of eating and drinking but of righteousness and peace and joy in the Holy Spirit." Sometimes we are offended because we see the world as obtaining possessions, and we lash out at others who place barriers to achieving those possessions. It's necessary to accept that life is more than just what things you see or desire. What you have allows you to fulfill your purpose. That very thing is your life, and you owe it to the Creator who makes it possible to obtain.

So is it offensive that God is in absolute control, that the Father is sovereign? The air we breathe and the water we drink can be taken away at a moment's notice. Some see that as offensive because they believe the sun rises and sets on their command. Here is a wild concept: suppose God decided to turn down the oxygen in the atmosphere by 60 percent; it belongs to the Creator to do so as He pleases. In Genesis we find that, on God's command, the water overtook the earth and all the people drowned except a family of eight (Genesis 7). God allows us to be on the earth even though we offend Him first with our actions. In the Old Testament, we see in Psalm 94:2 (ESV), "Rise up, O judge of the earth; repay to the proud what they deserve!" And yet, because of grace, we are allowed to grow beyond our offense and redirect our path.

Man and woman, and their offspring, are made in the image of God (Genesis 1:27). If it pleases you to bless or curse, why is your choice to curse rather than to bless? Is it your understanding of the gifts bestowed upon you? What a blessing your child is to you that you were trusted with taking them from newly entering the world to adulthood. As difficult as it may be at times, it's better for you to ask for help than to offend. The child suffers, yes—and needs healing. More than that, God is offended and expects reconciliation. In 2 Corinthians 5:20 (ESV), we read, "Therefore, we are ambassadors for

Christ, God making his appeal through us. We implore you on behalf of Christ, be reconciled to God."

In business, in your home, and in the community, you are an ambassador for Christ. At no time are you able to alleviate this position for convenience to apply offense. The very nature of reconciliation is to coexist harmoniously with God and therefore with others. Trying is not the same as doing. To reconcile exemplifies maturity, morals, and values at the forefront of your worldview; it is easier not to offend.

Chapter 11

Breathe—Don't You Dare Hold Your Breath

Unlike others, you may believe you're at a place in life where you can just tough things out. Along your journey you hold your breath, dig in, and accept the consequences of what happens because you don't feel in control of many areas of your daily life. Remember that being out of control in different aspects of your life does not equate to permanent defeat. We must hold fast to what is possible.

Questions:

- Why is this stage of life so intense?
- How can you be sure that you are seen?
- Who allows you to breathe?

All concepts, as you seek advice, are necessary for review quantitatively because you are deciding what to exclude. The quality of such information emerges once you have the best understanding. It's impossible to accept a foreign concept unless you see how connected it is to other concepts within a certain discipline. With that, it's necessary to see the concepts work in concert with people you believe in or admire. The concept needs to feel holistic and relevant to how you view the world. Otherwise, it's useless. You can take a breath because you see the value.

Unfortunately, many people see the world as something to combat daily, and therefore seeking advice is just a part of life. Others think of the world around them and accept that whatever happens is okay—they believe they will get through it. While both ideas, and others, are appropriate points of view, the question you inherently deal with is the level of daily combat and whatever happens as a result. Too many times it's overwhelming even if you can apply the advice you seek.

For example, now that you finally understand your uncle or manager's advice, you sit and reflect on how to apply it and the intensity of the results. No one desires to hear that their marriage or how they take care of their aging parents is wrong. Admit to yourself that you're not on top of everything. Those who do admit it are better at seeking advice and applying it. If you are a person who only seeks advice when it seems you will get support for what you want to do already, then you probably deny the intensity of the situation. And you're likely not going to apply it anyway.

Why wait to get started on applying advice? Is it ever going to be the best time for you? Your family is waiting for you, as the leader, to make the first move. Coworkers may be reluctant; however, they might follow your lead as they see you get results. Those on your team expect that you are seeking advice from other people in the C-suite and from coaches, gurus, seniors, entrepreneurs, and ministers.

The first thing to remember, considering the intensity of a situation, is not to deny that you are connected to a greater world and others have information to help you. "Plans fail for lack of counsel, but with many advisers they succeed" (Proverbs 15:22, NIV). The people around you are not counting solely on your expertise; they are basing their next life's moves on the wisdom of those around you too.

When you experience life's difficulties, you need someone to offer advice to keep you believing that what's next is truly possible. More so, you need to believe it is for you to win. As you look around at the roller coaster of life, the desire is that there be more highs than lows. To believe that winning is possible, we offer such hope to others—more highs than lows. No one wants to live their lives in perpetual expectation.

These are the times to accept that life is a journey, and this journey has several destinations. Graduating from school, obtaining a career, marriage, birth of children, getting a promotion on the job, and taking care of aging parents are examples that mark destinations. How many of those have been done by someone else you know? Is it foolish for you to lack judgment because you didn't seek to understand a better way (Proverbs 15:21)? So is the intensity because of pride?

When the aforementioned destinations in life become intense, it can be like fighting a war. "Plans are established by seeking advice; so if you wage war, obtain guidance" (Proverbs 20:18, NIV). That means you are aware of what is coming, and you prepare. Yes, of course, sometimes you're dealing with the aftermath. You plan for that too. Cleaning up afterward is a part of the entire plan. You can't send troops off to war and not expect them to return to your shores without proper medical attention for the body and mind. The same goes for your family. If there is home theft, for example, you must allow the children to grieve and check on them a month later, and then a few months after that.

Solitude is necessary because it allows you to reflect along the journey so that you give the proper context to whatever life offers you. It doesn't mean you walk away from your life; it means seeking counsel and spending time to make sure you understand it. Take a breath and realize the advice may be good for now or in the future. Too often people accept advice and move on it without considering a plan on how to use the advice. At any time you are unsure, ask someone else about how to keep going as you work out the plan. "Better was a poor and wise youth than an old and foolish king who no longer knew how to take advice" (Ecclesiastes 4:13, ESV). Never stop moving forward with a solution, even if you have to take a different road.

While working through your life's journey, you will sometimes feel alone. Though these feelings can be intense, realize you are never alone. The planet is full of people who experience what you experience (1 Corinthians 10:13). A support group that offers better insight for longer-term problems may be helpful. It's the same as getting advice and learning how to apply it from family or friends. Many times, support groups take the form of something formal. Other times, they are less formal because there's a need for you to feel relaxed. Either way, the outcome is the same. First listen, observe, and then apply what you acquire. Remember, the expectation is that you are there to obtain a better way for your journey.

Then why the intensity, you may ask? Who is benefiting from this amount of struggle? In James 1:2 (ESV), we note, "Count it all joy, my brothers, when you meet trials of various kinds." It means that you are worthy of proving yourself. Yes, it feels like something else—possibly even hate. You may believe that your coworkers hate you or your family has decided to abandon you. Once more, it may feel like nothing ever goes according to your plan. Remember, it takes a lot of strength to move forward. Placing one foot in front of the other can seem impossible. Though it's difficult, this is a time for you to get proof of your strength to endure in faith with your Creator (James 1:3).

Looking at history, we see that others face problems and are left in a struggle for their lives. That is the fallen world. Call on others for help, seek the wisdom of God, and prepare to apply the wisdom (James 1:5-8). You are seen through a clean lens because of salvation, and that makes you worthy. The reason to keep going is to seek others who need help like you. We share the basic needs of water, food, clothing, and shelter, and those things we generally can provide easily for others. If you find you are waiting for wisdom to move forward, that's where you start. Do so with fervor and patient understanding.

Others need you, and they are stuck in a place where you will be or have been. As you share, you will learn what you can use and what you can give to someone else. Through this interaction, you are seen. The people in your world have many reasons to push you away. With your determination to help others, you will help them feel seen, and in return you will feel the same. Know this: "Let each of you look not only to his own interests, but also to the interests of others" (Philippians 2:4, ESV). Being strong enough to help someone else reminds us that in our tough times, someone is willing to help us too. "We who are strong have an obligation to bear with the failings of the weak, and not to please ourselves" (Romans 15:1, ESV). When you spend more time showing love for your neighbor, it allows you to view the world as something you can bear.

There are times when you will want someone to come and rescue you. The world gives you so many reasons to expect it. You see people winning, and it seems you are owed the same. What we are "owed" does not always look the same for everyone. Yes, respect and honor are what a father desires from his family and coworkers. The expectation of basic decency when interacting with others is relevant to most cultures. Put discourse on the table; it is only proper to expect the same in return. So you change and place on the table harmony and trust, respect and decency—your investment will return to you exponentially.

The proper worldview considers the time before you as much as the time to come. Your mark in the world is more than giving something for a return. What you will receive is the benefit of living a life that honors selflessness versus selfishness. God does not need us for Him to exist. Although many promote that God is a creation of man, it is no contest as we view the universe God created. Acts 17:25 illuminates that the Creator does not require help from any human. God gives the breath you require, provides for the life you relish, and bestows upon you all your abilities and talents. Consider a worldview that honors that understanding. Breathing is a gift from the Holy Spirit even to those who do not believe.

You will not have all the answers to every question (Daniel 12:9, Revelation 10:4). What you can count on is the final answer. Loving God means God knows you (1 Corinthians 8:3). We expect to understand everything, and so we search with the possibility of disappointment. What we must realize is that everything we understand already has limitations. How does that help in your daily life? You were designed to seek answers. Cleverly and relentlessly you pursue, and still you will find more information that appeals to yet another level. Acceptance of that reality is joyful. The benefit is that you can relax because there are so many answers to the various questions; and yet there is more to discover and then complete rest.

Our Creator provided faith as a reason to seek more. God has settled the arguments before they begin. Colossians 2:4 shines a light on the intelligibility of a Creator giving reason to people to deconstruct what may seem plausible. As you seek more, you may get off-course. That is not an excuse to stop. Take time to plan and reassess as you act upon the advice. The warning of the Creator is this, "See to it that no one takes you captive by philosophy and empty deceit, according to human tradition…" (Colossians 2:8, ESV).

Anyone can provide advice. Test it. What are the roots of their advice? James 1:5-6 (ESV) offers this idea, "If any of you lacks wisdom, let him ask God, who gives generously to all without reproach, and it will be given him. But let him ask in faith, with no doubting, for the one who doubts is like a wave of the sea that is driven and tossed by the wind." Steadfast determination will compile reasonable advice. Advice without an overarching worldview that is coherent and plausible to all leaves out too many who share the same planet. You are bound by what your neighbor does or does not do. It doesn't mean we act as a monolith.

In response to those neighbors or housemates, do not seek advice to prove you're right or that someone else is wrong. Take a breath and remember to ask for advice because you are seeking a better way. Colossians 2:2-3 (ESV) clarifies, "That their hearts may be encouraged, being knit together in love, to reach all the riches of full assurance of understanding and the knowledge of God's mystery, which is Christ, in whom are hidden all the treasures of wisdom and knowledge." Being knit together with coworkers and neighbors means you work on what you understand will help us all, big or small. Working together harmoniously means we breathe easier.

Chapter 12

Truth—Narrowing the Wide View

Time is given for you to grow in wisdom so that you can reconcile yourself to a greater understanding. There's more than what we interact with daily, however much it takes over our mental picture of the world. The façade is a belief that we are given time to achieve, and that often means increasing fear and going into survival mode. That is how desire takes over versus growing in knowledge and wisdom. Too many replace their understanding of "needs" for what they want. Interactivity with others needs a foundation, a reliable foundation. For example, we share gravity and the sun, and that both are a constant. And, as recorded history will expose, we know what to expect concerning gravity. Although it can be manipulated as with an airplane or other projectiles, gravity is a truth we all share. No one expects gravity to stop suddenly and a new reality to exist. If one does, they are not looking at the consistency of all points that make gravity the truth for us all.

Questions:

- What is truth?
- Do you expect it?
- Is it necessary to be dedicated to the truth?

Searching for truth, you realize that many different cultures share some commonalities. They are both set in—stable, and yet an evolving reality. Taking a different look, you realize that it is the will of the people to evolve what they consider to be true above what is true. The hope of truth is that we accept that when confronted it is obvious to everyone. However, because of our deceptions, either culturally or from parents, friends, and community, the truth is distorted.

Can each of us have our own version of the truth? To answer that question, consider another: How long would it take you to say "hello" to all of your coworkers if all of us had our own version of morning greetings? The truth by its nature has to be limited. Touched by any disfigurement of language, hopes, dreams, aspirations, simulations, thoughts, or theories, it no longer holds its exclusivity. For something to be true, it continually must exist for all people in the past, present, future, and the ever-present now (the spiritual realm).

For example, suppose a country recognized their male children as royalty by the age of twelve, and any neighboring country had to acknowledge it or suffer. Before such a country grew large enough on the world stage, it was of no consequence to other countries. Why? It was easy to ignore them and live in peace. In this scenario, let's say the country with twelve-year-old dignitaries grows, and soon they have over a million who have a greater desire to show what a true crowned ruler can do. World history shows that many kings and emperors are unlikely to subject themselves to headship and thus they want to conquer. Is it worthy of any neighboring country to acknowledge those newly crowned now? The nature of the world's culture changes because of the power of such a country with a million in one country with such power. The degree of peace, on planet Earth, depends on everyone's ability to share in the truth of such a country. With a force behind the truth (or supposed truth), everyone will have to deal with it.

This brings me to my next point: None of us is the standard-bearer for truth. Meaning, no human being such as you or me corners the market. However, there has to be a standard-bearer for the truth. To say *no one* has a monopoly on the truth begs the question: Is there anything left out of that statement? Answering in the affirmative means you have nullified such an objectionable point. If neither of us ever existed, the truth would remain. The truth does not depend on any of us to be the standard-bearer. Otherwise, the truth would waver from a bearer's point of maturity to an emotional experience. How could we depend on consistency during those events? Further, I would ask, how could we ever expect the truth to be the principle in freeing anyone (John 8:32)?

Fact: the truth is not subject to debate. There are really only two arguments we ever have, and they are:

- How do I feel about something?
- Who is in charge?

The debate comes up and objectifies the truth because of your feelings or your inability to allow someone else to grow as they take charge. A person's feeling, versus you allowing them to be in charge, makes a difference.

Taking the truth claim to a more common point of contention, consider the toilet seat debate. Quite often, the discussion is about more than just the position of the toilet seat. Here's the point of agreement: the restroom should be left at its best presentation for the next guest. Is that a true statement, or is it the best way to settle what one person declares contrary to another?

The truth is something everyone can share. Not just everyone in your home or your particular culture—everyone! When others can't share the truth you proclaim and rely on it to achieve peace, it's no longer the truth. Your version of the truth is not as relevant as the actual, measurable, empirically coherent, cognitive, and stable truth. Facts are inarguable. What is often contemptuous is what a person desires to be the truth or what they remember. Once more, that is "How do I feel?" or "Who is in charge?"

In your home, the same applies. Only one person is the leader, and that person has to have the final say. Yes, of course, that person will make mistakes. It's also notable to say that person will not have all the facts, and/or the facts may be tainted. That's why it's necessary to have discussions of consequence with your mate; you establish what is true. That includes taking notes so you come to an understanding that helps all involved. Using the above example, let's say your house has four sons and two daughters, with only one son under the age of twelve. How much are they entitled to rule the home as royalty, with the same expectation as the parents? The truth matters when resolving family and work conflicts because it's a place where everyone must live with the consequence. A house divided against itself cannot stand (Mark 3:24). As so, something has to be above any discourse.

Integrity is central to you as an employer, coworker, and one who follows another's lead. The hallmark of integrity is reliability when you are not under a watchful eye. You desire others to be honest about everything that concerns your income, things you pay for, and your aspirations—such as participating in sports or the community. No one is let off the hook. Yes, you know it will be necessary to forgive others. That doesn't mean their integrity can be in question concerning your daily affairs.

If your team is not playing because of forfeiture or because they are knocked out for the season, and you stop watching the sport, are you a fan of the sport or just of your team? The sport, not just your favorite franchise needs you. Is your integrity in question concerning your commitment to the sport? The franchise knows they can rely on you. Does the entire league? You expect others to come through even when the impact is not direct. That is the expectation of truth. Holding others accountable for what you are not willing to give hurts your integrity. And it disrupts a truth claim such as "I take care of my family"—when they can hardly find you. Taking care of a family financially goes hand-in-hand with taking care of them as a loving participant.

The truth in being a loving participant is vital in your UNIT, because we need others to help hold a home together. "Though one may be overpowered, two can defend themselves. A cord of three strands is not quickly broken" is worth mentioning again (Ecclesiastes 4:12, NIV). The fact is that when you commit you must say it not for the truth you understand at the moment but also for the future. If you can't, your integrity is in question. Ask yourself if you expect the truth. When you commit to something, others are asking you not just for what is present or seemingly present. They are asking in regard to the larger picture of a marriage or a working relationship—based on what is "normal" in your culture. The belief is that what you expect in the future, good or bad—either way—you are truly committed.

A working relationship is different from building a family. How well you are committed changes because of the relationship. That doesn't negate the integrity you expect to give or receive. Deuteronomy 24:14 (ESV) states, "You shall not oppress a hired worker who is poor and needy, whether he is one of your brothers or one of the sojourners who are in your land within your towns." Doing so brings into question your expectation of truth. You pay for a good pair of shoes from a store, and you expect the shoes to be worth what you paid. That's why the truth is something everyone must be able to share. It makes the world's relationships, big or small, work harmoniously.

James 1:22 (ESV) writes to us saying, "But be doers of the word, and not hearers only, deceiving yourselves." The consequence is that when everyone takes the truth and twists it to their advantage, chaos will naturally appear. The more people are dedicated to the truth, the more harmony appears. Peace is inevitable. You cannot separate truth from peace. The definition of love from 1 Corinthians (13:5-6, ESV) says that love does not insist on its way, nor is it resentful, and love rejoices with the truth. In a relationship, both people rejoice when they find common ground because to them it's now something they can share. It's reliable, and over time it becomes the expectation.

So how do you make sure the truth works on your behalf? First, let's consider a few questions. Are you allowed to know the truth of this world around you? Are you ready for the truth, even if you don't want to accept it or it's uncomfortable? These things must be explored in reconciling the truth. Also, ask who is the giver of truth and whether it's a gift that works on your behalf. Is it something you are willing to work toward daily? To do this, you have to let go of what you worship or idolize concerning your beliefs. It doesn't matter how long you held the belief or desire. Letting go so that the truth prevails is what matters from this moment forward. When you fight gravity, it eventually wins unless you refuel your aircraft and do regular maintenance. Fighting gravity doesn't eliminate it.

Here's a way to check your dedication to the truth. For one year, count the number of lies you tell. Don't let anyone else know what you are doing. It's an internal discussion concerning honesty. Over the year, how you count will likely evolve. What is most important in this exercise, other than telling yourself the truth, is that you complete the exercise and reflect upon how you decided what is a lie.

You must have dedication to the truth because it works in your favor over your lifespan. Right now, either as a moment of calm or as your day of peace becomes disrupted, the truth prevails and is powerful. That's why we see children plunder, workers revolt, spouses reveal, and neighbors destroy because of the pain they feel when the truth puts them in a predicament. Your best calculation is that when the truth comes, it settles everyone from further unrest. Experiential knowledge brings peace. It's the wisdom of our older family and friends that we use because they know how to settle unrests as much as they know who will stir it up.

Further, realize that the truth will continually change how you interact with the world around you. What you express can be heartfelt and assuredly what you remember as the events that took place. Yet living on purpose and acknowledging the future means stopping opposition to the truth. When you seek advice from another about a family issue or career move, you ask because you want the truth. Being dedicated to what you hear, even if painful, allows you to live freely. Try this: instead of asking what to do about a situation, ask what is your role concerning the situation. Listen for the truth. Wait and ponder on it. More understanding will come as your integrity builds, and you will have peace. That is what happens as the Savior sets the captives free and they get to know the truth (John 8:32, 3:17).

As we examine our understanding of the truth, we must consider the ancient writers of various texts. Why would so many write in such a manner as to discuss the human condition and provide such intense warnings concerning our behaviors toward each other? Moreover, the writers offer wisdom about changing our behaviors and package it in a holistic reverence for love, thereby providing purposeful living to consistently reconstruct our understanding of love.

Consider a worldview that the original Author created.

Topics in Future Volumes

1. Marriage—Tying Down the Nuts & Bolts
2. Validity of Your Feelings
3. Not My Friend
4. Anger Soup
5. Mom! The Unicorn Is Acting Weird
6. Cold-Hearted
7. You Need There to Be a God
8. The Purpose of Your Pastor
9. The Weight and Blessing of Children
10. Follow

A Brief Word about the Author

Marcus L. Davis, BSc.
Leadership & Ministry

Growing up in a mid-sized town, Marcus went to church regularly with his family. His mother participated in the choir and a gospel group, and the family frequently volunteered at church. Times spent with his dad often brought lessons about love and respect for others, including those in other countries. His father's actions also reminded Marcus that a dad is much more than a provider.

Throughout his life's experiences, Marcus realized that his hunger for the gospel, rooted in his youth, was more knowledge-driven than relational. After leaving the military, he pondered different belief systems and eventually landed at a church that included teaching about the Holy Spirit. The result allowed him to see more of what his mother and father's drive was about as they encouraged God during his youth.

Once his faith was solid, Marcus was called into ministry. Like many, he didn't initially accept the call but rejected it, as well as the encouragement of others. Eventually landing at the church mentioned above, he came to understand the interconnectedness of the gospel and the Holy Spirit in addition to the Christ he heard about as a child. This journey led him to obtain a ministry degree and speak at different ministry events. Working in audio/visual arts, healthcare, leading a multimedia ministry, and a stint as a board chair allowed Marcus to interact with different cultures, ages, and lifestyles. Today, as he continues to advise others about God and relationships, it is a pleasure to share what is at the center of this book.

Scripture References by Chapter

1. Making It Happen – Career and Personal Goals
   a. Colossians 3:23
   b. Colossians 3:24
   c. Psalm 4:11
   d. 1 Timothy 6:6
   e. Proverbs 15:22

2. Inner and Outer Declarations
   a. 2 Corinthians 3:17
   b. Proverbs 18:21
   c. Matthew 12:37
   d. Proverbs 4:7
   e. Philippians 4:7
   f. Isaiah 26:3
   g. Psalm 119:165
   h. Psalm 119:168

3. Intentional Listening
   a. Psalm 141:1
   b. 2 Peter 1:9
   c. Proverbs 10:23
   d. Proverbs 12:15
   e. James 2:18
   f. 1 Corinthians 12:12-31

4. Loving Hard
   a. Proverbs 10:1
   b. Proverbs 26:12
   c. Proverbs 27:17
   d. Proverbs 26:4
   e. Ephesians 4:26
   f. Zephaniah 2:3
   g. Ephesians 4:1
   h. 1 Corinthians 13:4-8
   i. Leviticus 19:34
   j. 1 Corinthians 10:23

5. Language – The Potency
   a. Genesis 25:19-34
   b. James 1:22
   c. James 3:10
   d. James 3:6
   e. Judges 4:4-10
   f. 1 Thessalonians 1:2
   g. Proverbs 15:4
   h. Colossians 4:6
   i. Matthew 5:16
   j. Ephesians 4:29
   k. Ephesians 5:4
   l. Proverbs 26:20
   m. James 3:8

6. Leading with the Arrogance of Ignorance
   a. Proverbs 4:7
   b. 1 Timothy 5:8
   c. Titus 1:16
   d. Hebrews 3:13
   e. Matthew 19:8

f. James 2:26
g. Proverbs 22:24-25
h. 1 Peter 3:7

7. Is Now Like Then – Can I Count on You?
   a. Joshua 3:1-4
   b. 1 Timothy 6:6
   c. Proverbs 19:1
   d. Proverbs 4:24
   e. Matthew 5:37
   f. Matthew 7:2

8. The People Around You
   a. Hosea 3:5
   b. Matthew 5:44
   c. Ecclesiastes 4:12
   d. 1 Corinthians 10:13
   e. Colossians 1:28

9. Money's Purpose
   a. 1 Timothy 6:9-10
   b. Romans 12:8
   c. James 2:16
   d. Deuteronomy 8:18
   e. Deuteronomy 26:10-11
   f. Genesis 3:1
   g. Matthew 6:21
   h. Ecclesiastes 9:11
   i. 1 Timothy 6:6-7
   j. Ephesians 4:28
   k. 1 John 3:17
   l. Proverbs 14:31

10. Picture Yourself as Offended
    a. Acts 2
    b. Romans 12:8
    c. Romans 14:9
    d. Ephesians 4:26
    e. Romans 14:17
    f. Genesis 7
    g. Psalm 94:2
    h. Genesis 1:27
    i. 2 Corinthians 5:20

11. Breathe – Don't You Dare Hold Your Breath
    a. Proverbs 15:22
    b. Proverbs 15:21
    c. Proverbs 20:18
    d. Ecclesiastes 4:13
    e. 1 Corinthians 10:13
    f. James 1:2
    g. James 1:3
    h. James 1:5-8
    i. Philippians 2:4
    j. Romans 15:1
    k. Acts 17:25
    l. Daniel 12:9
    m. Revelation 10:4
    n. 1 Corinthians 8:3
    o. Colossians 2:4
    p. Colossians 2:8
    q. James 1:5-6
    r. Colossians 2:2-3

— Scripture References by Chapter →

12. Truth – Narrowing the Wide View
    a. Mark 3:24
    b. Ecclesiastes 4:12
    c. John 8:32
    d. Deuteronomy 24:14
    e. James 1:22
    f. 1 Corinthians 13:5-6
    g. John 8:32
    h. John 3:17

The format of this book is intended to discuss and touch on several different aspects of personal relationships and working relationships and to promote self-reflection. Most important, it is designed to improve your foremost relationship with the concept of love.

"May you love well and live
outrageously for Christ."
—Marcus L. Davis

ISBN: 978-1-7378981-0-8
Marcus1Media.com

Live the life you desire by finding out what really matters to the world we share.

www.ingramcontent.com/pod-product-compliance
Lightning Source LLC
Chambersburg PA
CBHW032130090426
42743CB00007B/546